MICHAEL ARRIA

MEDIUM BLUE

BLUE

The Politics of MSNBC

MICHAEL ARRIA
MEDIUM BLUE
The Politics of MSNBC

Published by CounterPunch Books

CounterPunch
PO Box 228, Petrolia, California, 95558

ISBN 9780989763738

A catalog record for this book is available
from the Library of Congress.

Library of Congress Control Number: 2014933442

Printed and bound in the United States.

"It is our view that, among their other functions, the media serve, and propagandize on behalf of, the powerful societal interests that control and finance them. The representatives of these interests have important agendas and principles that they want to advance, and they are well positioned to shape and constrain media policy. This is normally not accomplished by crude intervention, but by the selection of right-thinking personnel and by the editors' and working journalists' internalization of priorities and definitions of newsworthiness that conform to the institution's policy."

-Edward S. Herman and Noam Chomsky, *Manufacturing Consent*

"I was just watching MSNBC, and they had a woman that used to work for me and a couple of other people on there, and they were talking about the Republican primary. And I was laughing. I said, 'Boy, it really has become our version of Fox.'"

-Bill Clinton

"We are not going to lay down, do an easy interview, and President Obama knows it. We're not here to be the voice of the administration. There are a lot of things we agree on, but there are no deals. They don't tell us what to say, we don't ask them to come on and then we'll give them a free ride. That isn't how it works. And that gives us a certain amount of integrity, and I think that's what our audience respects about us."

-Phil Griffin, MSNBC President

"If that's your best, your best won't do."

-Twisted Sister

TABLE OF CONTENTS

INTRODUCTION

There's a celebrated scene from Aaron Sorkin's *The Newsroom*, in which Jeff Daniels' character, news anchor Will McAvoy, is wedged between a Democrat and a Republican, on a particularly excruciating panel, to discuss the state of American politics. Bored with the entire ordeal, at one point, while staring into the crowd, he sees someone who reminds him of his beloved ex-girlfriend or, maybe, he hallucinates her existence. It's hard to say.

Whether real or imagined, the representational audience member ignites McAvoy's inner-liberal. McAvoy has already grown agitated with the host's appraisal of his image, a vanilla shill who refuses to ever rock the boat. At the end of the public discussion, a questioner asks the assembled pundits to explain why America is the greatest country in the world. The Democrat, of course, says, "Diversity and opportunity." The Republican, of course, says, "Freedom and freedom." McAvoy attempts to dodge the question, but when the host prods him for a response, he counters with a blazing curveball. He declares, to a shocked crowd, reaching for their camera-phones, that the United States is not, in fact, the greatest country in the world. He then launches into an epic progressive tirade, capping on his fellow guests and diagnosing the nation's many ailments, before concluding with a tribute to past glory.

"We sure used to be. We stood up for what was right," he tells the audience, "We fought for moral reasons; we passed and struck down laws for moral reasons. We waged wars on poverty, not poor people. We sacrificed, we cared about our neighbors, we put our money where our mouths were, and we never beat our chest. We built great big things, made ungodly technological advances, explored the universe, cured diseases, and cultivated the world's greatest artists and the world's greatest economy. We reached for the stars, and we acted like men. We aspired to intelligence; we didn't belittle it; it didn't make us feel inferior. We didn't identify ourselves by who we voted for in the last election, and we didn't scare so easy. And we were able to be all these things and do all these things because we were informed. By great men, men who were revered. The first step in solving any problem is recognizing there is one—America is not the greatest country in the world anymore."

The first time I watched this scene on YouTube, I knew I wanted to write a book about MSNBC. Yes, *The Newsroom* is a television drama and MSNBC is an actual network with real people working for it, but never before had I seen MSNBC's strain of contemporary liberalism articulated so brilliantly. The power of Sorkin's scene relied on so many consistent progressive assumptions: the problems that plague America are recent developments and the wars of yesteryear were less brutal and waged for noble reasons. *We* cultivated the "world's greatest economy" as a unit and weren't defined by a sense of exceptionalism.

Since positioning themselves as a liberal alternative to Fox, MSNBC has projected these assumptions to millions of people on a daily basis. It's an effective game for all kinds of reasons, not least of which being the false dichotomy it generates. On one side you have the big, bad evil fabricators of Fox and, on the other side, you have the apostles of factuality at MSNBC. This book explicitly rejects this Conservative vs. Liberal media narrative, a storyline that runs through so much press analysis. It is my position that the fundamental problem with American media isn't that it's too conservative or too liberal, but that it's directly connected to elite opinion and reflects those interests and concerns. This book assumes that you know a place like Fox is a terrible source for news. Yes, there have been various robust criticisms of Fox, many of them tremendously illuminating, such as Robert Greenwald's 2004 documentary *Outfoxed*. However, criticism of Fox is an altogether different animal. The exposures of the conservative media are, generally straightforward and often undeserving of rigorous analysis. Nonetheless, liberals frequently bite on the trolling, bothering to waste time and words on superfluous tasks like fact-checking Ann Coulter books. Fox is run by Roger Ailes, a man whose fingerprints cover the race baiting of George Bush's 1988 presidential campaign, and the originator of the Orchestra Pit theory of political analysis. As he tells it, "If you have two guys on a stage and one guy says, 'I have a solution to the Middle East problem,' and the other guy falls in the orchestra pit, who do you think is going to be on the evening news?"

For years now, Fox News has been beaming out images of people falling into orchestra pits, red meat for its rabid base, as well as the liberals who love to hate on it. Progressive books, like Eric Alterman's *What Liberal Media?*, add up the amount of television time allotted to those on the hard right, as opposed to the center-left, and conclude the entire operation is in the bag for the conservatives, but such analysis misses the point; the issue isn't politics, it's power. Deeper questions must be asked: What is the function of the media in the United States and who controls it? How progressive can a network ever truly be within the parameters of a corporate-run media with a bottom-line that can be, drastically, influenced by the American people? How much *disrupting* can a network like MSNBC ever really do?[1]

The late Alexander Cockburn had a go-to anecdote about arriving in America, after years in London. In England, the pubs were packed with journalists feeling horrible about their lot in life, dulling the shame of their chosen profession with alcohol. When he got to the States, he quickly realized that all the bars were empty. Where are the journalists, he wondered, until eventually realizing that the game here was played much differently. American journalists weren't racked by guilt, but possessed by a sense of self-importance bestowed upon them in journalism school and carried into blighted culture obsessed with farcical prizes. MSNBC has been referred to as, "Fox for Democrats", by Bill Clinton among others, and, yes, the network frequently defends the Obama administration in much the same way Fox defended Bush, constructing a narrative that continually lets the President off the hook. However, there's a crucial distinction that must be made: Fox was never designed to be about facts or objectivity; it was constructed as a propaganda outfit for a media with deep totalitarian strains. The people behind Fox understand narrative in a way that folks at MSNBC, or for that matter anyone in the liberal establishment media, never will. The cynicism of the right-wing machine is easily decipherable by anyone willing to read between the lines: watch Bill O'Reilly admit to Stephen Colbert that some of his outrage is an act, listen to Rush Limbaugh say he's glad the GOP lost the House because he was tired of shilling for bad legislation, or pay attention to Glenn Beck when he says, "If you take what I say as gospel, you're an idiot."

In contrast, an outfit like MSNBC is packed with true believers who preach the false hope of objectivity. It interests me as a network specifically because of this. Unlike a place like Fox, there is seemingly no coercion, no suggestion that its pundits don't completely believe everything they say. There is no MSNBC equivalent to Glenn Beck, no rodeo clown occasionally in on the joke. Everyone working for the station seems to believe that they operate without restriction, often defining themselves as independently minded journalists attempting to squash the lies of a deceptive media.

The story of how it got to this point, how the station became liberal, isn't much of a story at all. There's no basis behind the station's liberalism beyond ratings. The tale begins during the summer of 2005. Former MSNBC host Keith Olbermann delivered a "special comment" at the end of his program, taking the Bush administration to task for their horrible reaction to Hurricane Katrina. The comments were hardly controversial, the public admiration Bush had garnished as a result of the 9/11 attacks had already begun to dissolve, and anyone with a television set could decipher that his response to New Orleans was botched at best and callous at worst. During a telethon to raise money for the victims, rapper Kanye West famously declared that "George Bush does not care about black people," a sentiment which resonated with millions of people throughout the country. As a major American city was left to be destroyed, then essentially converted into a warzone by private contractors and the police, even Keith Olbermann, at that point simply a former sports broadcaster who delivered the news with jokes, was compelled to call out the administration. "This is not typically a newscast of commentary," he began, before letting Bush have it and declaring that, in the muck of New Orleans, someone might be able to find our government's credibility.

Although not earth-shattering to the American people, this was a very big deal for MSNBC. As Olbermann had pointed out, the shows didn't usually dole out commentary and, when they did, they typically operated from a Fox-like structure: the bloviating right-wing nutbag arguing with the ineffective Alan Colmes stand-in. For years, MSNBC seemed to have no idea what kind of network it wanted to be, but it certainly showed no inclinations that it was moving in a liberal direction. Birthed in 1996, by General Electric's and Microsoft's unit, the station ran third in a three-horse race, lagging behind CNN and Fox in any category that mattered, including coherence. In 2006, the *New York* Post ran a column wondering why MSNBC even still existed, a decade after its creation. "The running joke in TV news is Fox and CNN are news channels with websites," wrote `Don Kaplan, "but MSNBC is a website with a cable channel."

In an effort to, perhaps, balance out, unintentionally hilarious, programs like *Alan Keyes is Making Sense,* the network hired left of center media personality, Phil Donahue, who producers canned him in less than a year, citing poor ratings. Their reasoning seemed suspicious. At the time, Donahue's show had more viewers than any other program on the network. The actual basis for his dismissal presumably stemmed from his opposition to the Iraq War, which other hosts at MSNBC cheered on vigorously. "We were the only antiwar voice that had a show, and that, I think, made them very nervous," Donahue explained in an interview with Fox News, "I mean, from the top down, they were just terrified. We had to have two conservatives on for every liberal. I was counted as two liberals."

Donahue's popularity had also, apparently, irked *Hardball* host Chris Matthews. According to a *New York* magazine piece on MSNBC, from 2010, Matthews had developed a close relationship with former General Electric CEO Jack Welch (General Electric owned NBCUniversal until March of 2013, when Comcast bought it out completely), in addition to summering with NBC CEO Bob Wright. In 2002, *US News and World Report* ran a gossip item claiming that Matthews declared he would bring down the network if Donahue stuck around. After the story ran, Matthews apologized to Donahue, but never denied making the statement.

After nixing Donahue, MSNBC doubled down on their Conservatism, replacing him with the infamously batshit Michael Savage, a radio shock jock who ignited controversy after 9/11 by suggesting we kill 100 million Muslims. Savage was dismissed, shortly after being hired, for telling a homosexual caller to, "Get AIDS and die."

Needless to say, Olbermann's outburst of sanity was not what MSNBC had signed up for. Phil Griffin, an MSNBC producer who would go on to become the network's president in 2008, told Olbermann to knock it off. That's when things began to get interesting. Despite Griffin's skepticism of Olbermann's Katrina rant, it became an Internet sensation and slowly, but surely, the politics of the station began to codify before viewers' eyes. The following year, during the summer of 2006, Olbermann ended his show with a tirade against Secretary of Defense Donald Rumsfeld. "In what country was Mr. Rumsfeld raised?" wondered Olbermann, "As a child, of whose heroism did he read? On what side of the battle for freedom did he dream one day to fight? With what country has he confused the United States of America?" Olbermann had always signed off with Edward R. Murrow's famous phrase, "Good night and good luck," but this particular diatribe provided a compelling explanation for the selection.

> *Although I presumptuously use his sign-off each night, in feeble tribute, I have utterly no claim to the words of the exemplary journalist Edward R. Murrow. But never in the trial of a thousand years of writing could I come close to matching how he phrased a warning to an earlier generation of us, at a time when other politicians thought they (and they alone) knew everything, and branded those who disagreed: 'confused' or 'immoral.' Thus, forgive me, for reading Murrow, in full: "We must not confuse dissent with disloyalty,' he said, in 1954. 'We must remember always that accusation is not proof, and that conviction depends upon evidence and due process of law. We will not walk in fear, one of another. We will not be driven by fear into an age of unreason, if we dig deep in our history and our doctrine, and remember that we are not descended from fearful men, not from men who feared to write, to speak, to associate, and to defend causes that were for the moment unpopular. And so good night, and good luck."*

In retrospect, this was a defining moment for MSNBC; not only was Olbermann beginning to reinvent his media persona and emerging as a progressive icon, he was linking this kind of journalism with the Hollywood liberalism of the good old days; a brand was beginning to form.

In Illinois, something else was happening. An African-American Senator, who had delivered the only memorable speech at the DNC a couple years prior, was beginning the final lap of his political ascent. People whispering about a black President were beginning to seem less and less irrational. There was something magnetizing about this politician's story, an element to his demeanor and rhetoric that seemed to transcend the predictable banalities that Americans had come to expect from their elected officials. At a liberal author's book reading around the same time, I watched an older gentlemen ask if another star was on the horizon, "There's this guy," he said, "Barack Obama. He's got what JFK had."

This perfect, left-of-center storm was occurring during an interesting, yet largely misunderstood, time in our nation's history. Whenever people look back on the cataclysmic days of the Bush administration, they tend to cite all the horrible things he did: the occupation of Afghanistan, the invasion of Iraq, his response to Hurricane Katrina, tax-cuts for the most wealthy Americans, etc. Almost never discussed are the progressive victories of his second-term. Think Bush did a lot of horrible things? Just think of everything he *wanted* to do, but was unable to: privatize Social Security, pass an amendment banning gay marriage, invade Iran, invade Syria, and a myriad of other deplorable ideas, that were on the table for his second-term. Bush, of course, faced a vociferous backlash domestically. It was sizable enough to handcuff his second-round of political prerogatives; the GOP lost the House, the AFL-CIO rallied against his attempted budget cuts, an Iraqi journalist chucked a shoe at him, and a more skeptical political culture began to form. By the time of the 2008 Republican National Convention, George W. Bush was a troubling liability, beamed in briefly via satellite. After leaving office, he retired to Crawford, to paint pictures of dogs.

Rumblings about MSNBC's preference to Obama began to sprout up during the 2008 Democratic primaries. At the time, it didn't seem like anything beyond the usual Democratic Leadership Council sniping, with supporters of the Clinton-machine like Governor Ed Rendell voicing their concerns. According to Lanny Davis, a former advisor to both Clintons, he confronted longtime MSNBC host Chris Matthews about his Obama-obsession in public. Matthews had infamously declared that, "I have to tell you, you know, it's part of reporting this case, this election, the feeling most people get when they hear Barack Obama's speech. My, I felt this thrill going up my leg. I mean, I don't have that too often." After Hillary Clinton pulled an impressive surprise victory in the New Hampshire primary, Matthews appeared on MSNBC's *Morning Joe* to explain to the American people that, "I'll be brutal, the reason she's a U.S. senator, the reason she's a candidate for president, the reason she may be a front-runner is her husband messed around. That's how she got to be senator from New York. We keep forgetting it. She didn't win there on her merit."

According to Davis, Matthews promised he would try to do better, but the tone of the station remained the same, and its focus on Obama began to seem like more than a Hillary campaign preoccupation. After he beat Clinton, MSNBC seemed to hitch its future on the Democratic candidate, even changing its on-air slogan to "The Power of Change", in homage to the candidate's. According to a study conducted by the Project for Excellence in Journalism, negative stories about Barack Obama comprised a mere 14% of the station's coverage, while negative stories about, his Republican opponent, John McCain made up 73%.[2]

For their efforts, MSNBC was granted access to our leader. In 2009, Keith Olbermann and Rachel Maddow were among several people invited to the White House to attend an off-the-record briefing. MSNBC, after years of being nothing but a beltway punch line and repository for prison documentaries had, finally, arrived.[3]

This book doesn't possess a hidden agenda. It's an attack on MSNBC from the left, an attempt to highlight and track the problematic ties between the network and America's ruling class. The message of MSNBC, juxtaposed with the propaganda of Fox, forms a false dichotomy and leads Americans to believe a strong debate is gripping the nation. Naturally, misguided discussions about civility begin to break out. Is Fox being too hard on Democrats? Is MSNBC being too hard on Republicans? Can't we all just get along? People, frequently, lament the increase in partisan rancor and pine for the good old days, when Tip O'Neill and Ronald Reagan ate lunch together. There is, of course, a striking irony to this gripe:

yes, perhaps, things have gotten more cantankerous, but the two major political parties have never been more closely aligned when it comes to fundamental issues that impact our world. Pick any major one at random (trade policy, nuclear disarmament, the World Bank, IMF, WTO, the private prison boom, the "War on Drugs", corporate welfare, Israel, Cuba, drone policy, the global assassination program, etc.) and think about what passes for a distinction between the two camps. Yes, MSNBC occasionally interviews informative guests, and hosts spirited debates, but, overall, it does very little to transcend the aforementioned, and accepted, gridlock of Washington. In many ways, it is very much part of the problem.

MADDOW'S WORLD

"I'm undoubtedly a liberal, which means that I'm in almost total agreement with the Eisenhower-Era Republican Party platform."

-Rachel Maddow

Keith Olbermann was suspended in 2010 after it was revealed that he made donations to a few Democratic political candidates.[4] Most glaringly, he had sent Raul Grijalva money, shortly after the Arizona Representative had appeared on his show. Olbermann's actions violated MSNBC's contribution policy, which requires network approval before any such donation is made. A couple months after Olbermann returned from his suspension, MSNBC ended their contract with the host. Later reporting detailed that a friction had developed between Olbermann and the station. According to a *New Republic* story about MSNBC from 2013, Phil Griffin openly criticized the popular talk-show liberal: "To colleagues, he made fun of the way he wore his pants. He joked that he was a virgin. He employed every cutting expletive he knew and even invented a couple."[5]

The loss of Olbermann paved the way for the meteoric rise of Rachel Maddow, a former Rhodes Scholar, whose interest in broadcasting led her to a gig at the ill-fated *Air America*, a progressive radio network founded during the Bush years in a misguided attempt to balance out the conservative-dominated medium. Popularized by the involvement of comedian, and current Minnesota Senator, Al Franken, *Air America* ended up standing as a symbol for the limitations of anti-Bush sentiment, a variation of resistance that frequently failed to address the systematic issues that plagued the American political system.

For instance, during the height of the Iraq War, there was barely any discussion, on *Air America,* about a full troop withdrawal. Criticisms of America's attack tended to focus on the corrupt nature of the occupation or the "mismanagement" of the Bush administration's military policy. This outlook reflected the view of, the 2004 Democratic candidate, John Kerry, who believed that the key to success in Iraq was an increase in troop levels. Maddow was one of the only voices, at *Air America,* who frequently brought up the topic of withdrawal and for her efforts she, well, I'll let listener John Walsh tell it...

"When I called Randi Rhodes (Air America afternoons) and managed to bring up the question of withdrawal she went ballistic, yelling that, now that 'we' were there, 'we' could not simply leave. She then shouted that I was a 'creep,' and off the air I went. I called Sam Seder and Janeane Garafalo (Air America evenings), and the screener suggested that Sam 'probably did not want to discuss withdrawal.' But I got on anyway after telling the screener that he was serving as a censor, and I asked Sam and Janeane why they did not discuss the withdrawal option. They went berserk, accusing me of not listening "enough," and off the air I went amidst their shouting. There are some exceptions to the pro-war stance on Air America or I should say there were. Liz Winstead, Rachel Maddow and Chuck D. used to have the mid-morning show where there was some discussion of withdrawal. [Rap luminary Chuck D was one of only two black hosts at the station, but was replaced by tabloid talk show host Jerry Springer. When an organization called Coalition for a Just Cincinnati protested the move, outside his show, Springer called the cops on them.] Liz, who is a talented comedian and co-creator of the Daily Show, disappeared mysteriously without explanation. Maddow with co-host Chuck D, lasted a bit longer. One day Maddow ran a segment stating that withdrawal from Iraq should be THE main point of discussion on the left. It was clear that she favored withdrawal in opposition to her guest, the strange and devious Paul Rieckhoff of Operation 'Truth,' who also calls for 'staying the course.' (She also challenged Ed Rendell, the Democratic governor of Pennsylvania, for supporting an anti-choice candidate to run against Rick Santorum for Senate, despite the existence of a pro-choice majority in Pennsylvania. Embarrassed and befuddled, Rendell said on air he was put up to this by Senate leaders, including H. Clinton and Charles Schumer.) Now Chuck D has also disappeared, and Maddow has gone quietly into the night, quite literally, with a one-hour show at 5 am. The final song on her last mid-morning show was: 'What Would you Give in exchange for your Soul"?[6]

One wonders if Maddow perceived the bump as suspicious but the setback proved to be temporary. She eventually gained an additional hour of programming, and an evening slot. She also became a regular panelist on MSNBC's *Tucker*, a program hosted by conservative commentator Tucker Carlson. Griffin didn't believe that Maddow looked the part (openly-gay and geeky, she didn't scream "cable news") but Carlson went to bat for her and his instinct proved correct. After filling in for Olbermann a few times, the network began to see a real star beginning to blossom. In a *New York Times* article titled, "Now in Living Rooms, the Host Apparent," Griffin admitted that, "At some point, I don't know when, she should have a show. She's on the short list. It's a very short list. She's at the top."[7] In August of 2008, she was given her own program.

The debut of *The Rachel Maddow* show was met with positive reviews. In Maddow, many felt as if they were watching an everyday person deliver the news, not some synthetic dolt reading off a teleprompter. As a review of her new program proclaimed, "Suddenly on the net everyone was talking about their new girl crush. Here was someone on television with whom they connected; who, in the cosy familiarity that comes from being on screen five nights a week, they imagined that they could be friends with. They liked the fact that she can mix a mean cocktail, never shops for clothes and is more interested in her pick-up truck than lunchtime Botox injections."[8] What's more, Maddow's arc was coinciding with Barack Obama's, the Illinois Senator who had, somehow, managed to trump the mammoth Clinton-machine and now eyed an old, erratic GOP candidate with a despised VP selection. If liberals believed that Obama was a hip community-organizer, aiming to correct the embarrassing reign of Bush, Maddow stood in as an ambassador for that change. No network had generated liberal stars during the early years of the Bush administration, not least because the Democrats were experiencing a paralyzing branding problem during this time. With the exception of doomed insurgents like Dennis Kucinich, the Democratic Party, under Bush, was muddled, boring, complacent, and forgettable; progressive media outlets, like *Air America*, reflected these ailments. In contrast, Barack Obama's popularity transcended politics, it created a space for disappointed liberals to project their own personal vision for the future upon the vague declaration of "Hope and Change." "I don't usually admire Sarah Palin," said Noam Chomsky, "but when she was making fun of this 'hopey changey stuff,' she was right; there was nothing there. And it was understood by the people who run the political system, and so it's no great secret that the US electoral system is mainly a public relations extravaganza... it's sort of a marketing affair." Shortly after Obama proved victorious in the 2008 election, he won *Advertising Age*'s marketer of the year award, beating out Apple. "I honestly look at [Obama's] campaign and I look at it as something that we can all learn from as marketers," said Angus Macaulay, Vice President of Rodale marketing solutions.[9]

The MSNBC brand, ignited by Olbermann and furthered by the election of 2008, had fully taken form with Maddow as its primary representative. Her crowning achievement would occur a couple years into her reign, when she challenged, chairman of Kentucky Taxpayers United, Rand Paul. Rand, the son of Texas congressman Ron Paul, was running as the Republican candidate, for one of Kentucky's Senate seats. Paul is, of course, a libertarian, a word that, like most political phrases, means almost nothing if not quantified. Many contemporary American libertarians have very little in common with Joseph Déjacque and often express political sentiments riddled with hypocrisy. Paul wants the government to get off your back and go fuck itself, unless you happen to be a woman, in which case the government reserves jurisdiction over your reproductive organs. Paul wants to cut foreign aid, but leave the $3 billion American taxpayers dole out to Israel every year alone because, security or something.

Yes, Paul's politics reflect a level of libertarian purity specifically wired to an imaginary Utopia of Hate in which individuals strive to screw each other over with bombastic levels of gusto. Paul's strict conformity to the tenets of free-market religious belief have, naturally, led him to embrace a number of comically horrid positions and one of the more bizarre is his view of the Civil Rights Act of 1964. He's against it. To Paul, the idea of forcing a business to stop segregating is akin to the government prohibiting you from burning leaves in your backyard. After all, this used to be a free country. Paul claims that, if alive, he would have gladly joined the struggle of Civil Rights and marched alongside Martin Luther King, but the most radical Civil Rights legislation of all time? "It's not about race relations," contended Paul, "it's about controlling property ultimately."

During an interview with Paul, which aired on her show, Maddow zeroed in on this problematic point, presumably with visions of David Frost's Nixon interviews dancing through her head. Maddow claims she had other questions, but she only asked him about the Act. She justified her focus by explaining to Paul, "The reason that this is something that I'm not letting go even though I now realize it would make the conversation more comfortable to move on to other things and I think this is going to be a focus for national attention on you, I guess until there's at least clarity on it, is that issue of the tenth, not the nine, but the tenth out of the 10 portions -- proportions of the -- the tenth of the Civil Rights Act that you would want to have discussions about. As I understand it, what you're saying, that's the portion of the Civil Rights Act that said you can't actually have segregated lunch counters here at your private business..."

Paul responded, "Well, I think it's interesting because the debate involves more than just that, because the debate also involves a lot of court cases with regard to the commerce clause. For example, right now, many states and many gun organizations are saying they have a right to carry a gun in a public restaurant because a public restaurant is not a private restaurant. Therefore, they have a right to carry their gun in there and that the restaurant has no right to have rules to their restaurant. So, you see how this could be turned on many liberal observers who want to excoriate me on this. Then to be consistent, they'd have to say, oh, well, yes, absolutely, you've got your right to carry your gun anywhere because it's a public place. So, you see, when you blur the distinction between public and private, there are problems. When you blur the distinction between public and private ownership, there really is a problem. *A lot of this was settled a long time ago and isn't being debated anymore.*"

The emphasis is mine. The victory was Maddow's. Her interview with Paul was heralded as a great liberal takedown of an evil conservative that wanted to bring back segregation. Following Maddow's takedown, there was a pronounced focus on Rand Paul's eccentric brand of nuttiness, including a *Boston Phoenix* story calling for him to withdraw from the race, anticipating irreparable harm to the GOP: "You can't go back and re-open that -- especially when you're the party with a highly dubious reputation on diversity and tolerance already. It's a potential disaster, and the party needs to contain it by quarantining themselves from Dr. Paul."

Despite a great number of Rand Paul denunciations, there was very little liberal analysis of, his opponent, Jack Conway, who simply possessed the droll variation of nuttiness typically associated with American politicians. Conway supported the Bush tax cuts, approved of the attack on Iraq, and was even against decriminalizing marijuana for medical purposes, but MSNBC never bothered identifying Conway's deficiencies as possible reasons for Paul's impressive surge. By the same token, they didn't seem very interested in the resonance that a figure like Paul might have with the segment of the population concerned about the destruction of Constitutional rights. Maddow's interview pegged Paul as a symbol of heinous racism, a figure for the Tea Party to embrace while they waved monstrous signs demanding that Obama produce his birth certificate.

The farce was brilliantly filleted by Alexander Cockburn, who wrote, "Here's Maddow, brandishing the Civil Rights Act of 1964, as though this is the only matter worth considering in the forthcoming race between Rand Paul and the Democrat, an awful neo-liberal prosecutor, Kentucky's current attorney general, Jack 'I'm a Tough Son-of-a-Bitch' Conway. Between Conway and Paul, who one in the U.S. Senate would more likely be a wild card – which is the best we can hope for these days – likely to filibuster against a bankers' bailout, against reaffirmation of the Patriot Act, against suppression of the CIA's full torture history? Paul, one would have to bet, and these are the votes that count, where one uncompromising stand by an outsider can make a difference, unlike the gyrations and last-ditch sell-outs of Blowhard Bernie Sanders. Liberals love grandstanding about what are, in practice, distractions. You think the Civil Rights Act of 1964 is going to come up for review in the U.S. Senate?"[10]

Paul was, of course, elected despite the Maddow dust-up and, in March of 2013, Cockburn's words proved prescient. The Kentucky senator launched a filibuster to block the nomination of John Brennan as Director of the CIA, citing his connection to the Obama administration's, possibly illegal, drone program. The spectacle was predictably filled with a distracting level of nonsense, as most events featuring a multitude of GOP speakers tend to. After, Florida Senator Marco Rubio quoted Pittsburgh-rapper Wiz Khalifa, the proceedings seemed to devolve into the stuff of Pynchon novel. Paul's resistance to Obama's drone program was tremendously truncated; he fixated on the idea of an American being assassinated in an outdoor café, while saying very little about the people of Pakistan, many of whom have been terrorized consistently by the devices since Obama became President, despite living in a country that is, technically, an American ally in its "War on Terror."

That evening, some on the left took to Twitter to wonder where the Democrats were. Why was Paul, a caricature of libertarian wackiness, willing to challenge the president on this crucial issue, while liberals sat on their hands? Surely, some Democrat could articulate a criticism of the CIA's drone program that transcended the limitations of Paul's, people speculated, but whom did progressives expect to show up? Elizabeth Warren, supporter of brutal sanctions on Iran and AIPAC mouthpiece? Barbara Boxer, who didn't even possess enough courage, to vote on the nomination? Al Franken, who voted for Brennan? Bernie Sanders ended up voting against Brennan, but a filibuster over drones? The self-described "socialist" has worked, in conjunction with local politicians, to outsource political control of his state's economy to military contractors.

At a certain point, liberals began waxing nostalgic for the late, often great, Senator Paul Wellstone. But why should we assume Wellstone would have joined a filibuster regarding this kind of overreach? He voted for the Patriot Act, after all. The only Senator who voted against that piece of legislation was Russ Feingold, who lost his Wisconsin Senate seat to radical right-winger Ron Johnson in 2010, in a campaign that Obama's enthusiastic base barely paid any attention. Ron Johnson actually showed up to at Paul's filibuster, seemingly unaware of what a drone was, and launched into an unintentionally comical rant about the perception of the GOP in our culture. Johnson was the proverbial cherry on a sundae of perplexing manure. Paul had, perhaps accidentally, ignited a national discussion on drones, but Democrats demonstrated no willingness to become involved. Despite his stance on the Civil Rights Act of 1964, Paul did, indeed, prove to be a wild card which, as Cockburn tragically predicted, was as good as anyone could hope for nowadays.

Paul's concern about drones, the space he opened up, and the missed opportunity of progressives was, seemingly, less important to Maddow than his stance on a piece of legislation from the 1960s and there's ample evidence to suggest why. On a Howard Stern appearance in 2012, Maddow told the shock-jock that drones, "Don't change the politics of [war] that much." This is an interesting reading of a military development that many regard as unprecedented. As journalist Sean Fenley blogged, "In reality, however, the politics have changed markedly because of the US military's use of their stable/panoply of death-inducing/mass immolating drones. And it is, moreover, exceedingly unclear what is meant by Maddow's comments as, for example, families have embarked upon lawsuits against the US government for innocents, non-terrorists, and non-combatants — who have been unceremoniously snuffed out— by the legally hazy, and decidedly unmanned aerial drones."[11]

This is an especially intriguing comment from Maddow because she is quite tuned into the subject of foreign policy. She is the author of *Drift,* a critique of how America goes to war. The book certainly has some compelling moments, but a problematic thesis emerges that is predicated on the allure of legality. To Maddow's mind, the definitive problem with American foreign policy is its current disregard for debate. She cites Reagan's secret war against Nicaragua as an example of the government run amok, then educates her readers on the much cheerier days of the Gulf War. In that conflict, George H.W. Bush obtained consent from Washington, and established an impressive coalition of countries primed to remove a brutal dictator from power. ""Agree or disagree with this outcome," wrote Maddow, "the system had worked. Our Congress had its clangorous and open debate and then took sides. We decided to go to war, as a country."[12]

But what does it mean that the system *worked* and what difference does it make to civilians in other countries, who find themselves on the receiving end of American bombs? As Charles Davis wrote in a review of Maddow's book, "If the system was working as late as 1991, albeit in fits, that raises a pretty big question: is it really worth saving? The history of the US is characterized by near-constant military actions and threats of war, including during the first century and a half when all those constitutional checks and balances were purportedly operating at full capacity. With "Jeffersonian prudence" holding sway, the US government fought major wars with Britain, Mexico and Spain. It militarily occupied Haiti, Nicaragua and the Philippines. Long before Reagan purportedly created the imperial presidency, US presidents were authorizing the killing of hundreds of thousands of Vietnamese, Cambodians and Koreans."[13]

Maddow's thirst for humanitarian intervention, complete with rhetorically impressive declarations and without the cowboy swagger that defined Obama's predecessor, was satisfied after the President decided to bomb Libya. "Whether or not you like this intervention in Libya, it's clear that the President's explanation for why it is justified matches what he said he would do with military force—what he would see as the justifiable use of the U.S. military," she told her audience. "It is clear that it matches what he said about that issue at the very start of his presidency, when in his first year as President, he accepted the Nobel Peace Prize."

Obama did say some things. For instance he said, "Some nations may be able to turn a blind eye to atrocities in other countries; the United States of America is different," a declaration that should have been delivered alongside a laugh track in various locations throughout the world, including Libya, a nation which has been on the wrong side of American aggression for decades; a thorn in the side of the Empire since Gaddafi took power, in 1969, and nationalized the country's oil supply.

"So the United States wants Gaddafi gone; the United States will not use military force to force him out," Maddow explained. "If Gaddafi is ousted, the U.S. will participate in efforts to stabilize Libya, but the U.S. will not lead those efforts. In the meantime, the United States will participate in an open-ended international intervention to stop Gaddafi, but the goal of that mission day-to-day and the timeline on which it will be carried out are, frankly, unknown. For all the clamoring here at home for Presidential communication to the nation on this, well, you got it, America—you got the clearest possible Presidential statement about the muddiest possible ongoing, indeterminate, international situation, otherwise known as a war. Discuss."

Maddow's ringing endorsement of NATO's attack on Libya set the tone for the entire network. (Initially, Chris Hayes opposed the intervention, but after the administration began beating the war drum to grease an attack against Syria, he mentioned, on Twitter, that he changed his mind on Libya.) Ed Schultz lobbed the most emotional case for attack; a populist conservative pundit turned populist liberal pundit and host of MSNBC's *The Ed Show.* Schultz' anti-Clinton politics took a progressive turn after he visited a Salvation Army cafeteria and he has been attempting to play the left-wing loudmouth role ever since, satisfying those perplexing progressives who pined for a Democratic Rush Limbaugh. (In 2011, he matched Limbaugh's revolting level of sexism, when he referred to Laura Ingraham as a "right-wing slut.")

When it came time to go to bat for another one of Obama's wars, Schultz laid out his perception of United States involvement in the most rhapsodic terms: "Whether or not we arm rebels, freedom fighters, whatever you want to call them, is a very hard decision, but I think we have to do it," reasoned Schultz. "Look, I am a Liberal, I am a Progressive. But that means that we need to stand behind people who want freedom. This isn't Bush talk; this is totally different from Iraq. It's totally different from any other situation, in my opinion. This is a situation where we have got a coalition that has come together and realized that Gaddafi is a terrorist. The President has gone on record saying that Libyan agents have killed Americans. That's all as an American I need to hear. Let's get it done. Let's arm these rebels; let's give them a chance to fight."

After Schultz' rousing Declaration of War, he welcomed, investigative reporter, Jeremy Scahill on his program, to discuss the issue. The conversation quickly became an impassioned debate, as Scahill beganw to pick apart the reality of what Schultz was calling for.

Schultz: Does this headline—how damaging is it to the President? The headline reads that the President sent CIA into Libya, what do you think?

Scahill: Well, the CIA operatives on the ground there are sort of engaged in an eHarmony dot COM or sort of, [uh, you know] dating service relationship with the rebels for the clandestine world. I mean, this is, as [as] Colonel Jacobs said, standard fare. What I think is of [of] more concern is the fact that there are certainly U.S. special operations forces units that are deployed already, secretly, inside of Libya that are painting targets for the air strikes. But, Ed, I have to say that the [the] scenario you're laying out—when you talk about arming the quote unquote "freedom fighters," it really evokes images of the disastrous dirty wars of the 1980s, I mean, the United States getting involved in what is effectively a Libyan civil war, a thousand or so rebels—

Schultz: It does.

Scahill: That don't have much military training, I mean, what you're advocating is [is] that Americans are going to have to be totally invested in [in in] one side of a civil war. The President stuck his neck out very far when he said that Gaddafi has to go. If the United States sends troops in there, and they would have to, as Colonel Jacobs said, if they're arming it, then we have a third full-on war, in addition to the covert wars that the President's waging in Yemen and Somalia and elsewhere on the Horn of Africa. I think a lot of military folks see mission creep in a big way here, Ed.

Schultz: Well, we have got a coalition put together, no question about it. We have got a willing coalition put together. Timing is everything. The circumstances surrounding this right now present us an opportunity to do justice on a man who the President says his agents have killed Americans.

Scahill: There's no question that Muammar Gaddafi—I'm sure that most of the entire world wants to see Muammar Gaddafi gone, but the fact is that Ali Abdullah Sale, the President of Yemen, is a murderous thug who has been sniper-shooting non-violent protesters, and he remains a close friend of the Obama Administration. The [the] dictatorship, the Khalifa family in Bahrain, [these are, these are] this is a corrupt monarchy and the only thing that we get out of them is hosting the fifth fleet there, so don't say anything about their violence. The message we're sending [*] to the world here is total hypocrisy.

Schultz: Well, wait a minute, the UN Security—but [but] the UN Security Council has not rendered judgment on the country. That you're talking about.

Scahill: Well, the fact, the fact of the matter is, Ed, that that UN Security Council resolution was the result of blackmail and cajoling on the part of the Obama Administration. A majority of the world's people represented on the Security Council, Brazil, uh, China, Russia, India they abstained, because they didn't want anything to do with taking sides in this civil war. That's the majority of the world's citizens represented in there.

Schultz: You're-you-you And [and] that's their call. That's their call. But they didn't [but they but they didn't but they didn't] stop it. Now—they didn't. They could—but China could have stepped up, the Rus—the Russians could have stepped up...There's no NATO, there's no NATO without the United States, there's no UN Security Council without the United States.

Schultz: They could have blocked this action in Libya, no question about it. Every situation is different, and Secretary Hillary Clinton has said just that, and the President's been very clear on it. We have a situation now to bring justice on a terrorist who has killed Americans. That's why I support this policy, that's why I support this move.

Scahill: Well Ed, this sounds a lot to me like Ollie North and the Iran Contras where you take a thousand people and call them freedom fighters.

Schultz: You can make any judgment you want. Jeremy, you can, you can, paint me any way you want.

Scahill: You're backing a thousand people, Ed. [Schultz laughs] Inside of a very large country, and, and, you're taking sides in a civil war. And what you're advocating is going to lead to more American deaths and hundreds of millions of dollars.

Schultz: You don't know that! You don't know that.

Scahill: Well it's already cost us 400 million dollars.

Schultz: Becau—because President Oba—I take President Obama's word for it that troops will not be engaged on the ground. I take [*] his word for it.

Scahill: Well, [well] what about he—

Schultz: Now, if he wants to hang me and my opinion out to dry [*] as an American, that's fine.

Scahill: OK, well...you know what President Obama has done, whose word you've taken, he didn't—

Schultz: My President Obama?

Scahill: He didn't clo—he didn't clo-Whose word you've taken—

Schultz: My President Obama? Is he your President too?

Scahill: Whose word you're taken, I said. He didn't close Guantanamo.

Schultz: Jeremy, is he you're Pres—wait a minute now, no you're not going to be at the water's edge [??], is he your President too?

Scahill: Of course he is. I'm an American; of course he's my President. I said 'the word,' you're saying you take his word for it. And—

Schultz: I do take his word for it.

Proceeding from Maddow's call for discussion, and Schultz's subsequent belief in Obama's words, it's important to take a deep look at what actually occurred in Libya, an intervention that faded from the headlines, soon after Qaddafi was captured and killed, but a country which reasserted itself into the political discourse after, US Ambassador to Libya, Christopher Stevens and three other Americans were murdered outside the embassy. Those tragic killings ended up igniting a media firestorm, which serves as a telling case study for how hollow the Fox/MSNBC dichotomy truly is. Republicans, and their preferred network, finally detected a foreign policy blunder from the Obama administration that could be exploited. The thousands of additional troops the President put in Afghanistan, the drone attacks that killed hundreds of innocent civilians, the targeted assassinations of American citizens, and the consistent application of the Espionage Act against those who dared share the Empire's secrets were not issues that the GOP could gain traction on. After all, most Republicans agreed with him on these policies.

However, the death of a US ambassador was an event that provided an opportunity to distinguish the GOP from the Democrats, while providing the possibility of a scandal that would take down the administration in the court of public opinion. After giving a speech blaming the ordeal on the Obama administration, Republican candidate, Mitt Romney tellingly walked away from the podium with a shit-eating grin on his face. The scandal never really stuck, beyond the segment of the population who believe Obama to be an inauthentic American, but MSNBC's response to the killings was quite telling. Rather than look back at their enthusiastic support of the Libyan intervention, and place it within the context of the ambassador's murder, they did little more than razz the right-wing for attempting to make hay over it. Nearly every show on the network ran multiple segments mocking Republicans for attempting to politicize the tragedy.

Lost in this bout of self-adulation was the analysis of a journalist like Vijay Prashad, journalist and author of the book *Arab Spring, Libyan Winter.* In a piece for *The Hindu*, Prashad put the tragedy within the context of the intervention, explaining how the two events were not mutually exclusive. If Fox had, what they perceived to be, a legitimate scandal to hold onto, then MSNBC had a legitimate war to grip. This tug-of-war complete obscured the crucial issues on the ground in Libya. "Benghazi entered the U.S. presidential campaign as a proxy for a debate over foreign policy between Obama and Romney," wrote Prashad, "Neither has taken honestly the consequences of the U.S.-led NATO intervention, and neither is capable of understanding the grave situation in Libya where certain militias act with impunity. A U.S. State Department document from August remarks that the Libyan government has acknowledged the problem of the Militias in torture and detentions, but it admits that the police and Justice Ministry are not up to the task of stopping them. On Tuesday, it sent out a text message on all cell phones, pleading for the militias to stop." The U.S. worries that Libya might become a 'failed state.' What is not recognized is that it is precisely the lack of seriousness toward accountability and law that fuel the failure of new institutions to emerge. Ambassador Chris Stevens was not the only victim of this lawlessness. He is one among many."[14]

As for those rebels that Ed Schultz was so eager to arm, they didn't turn out to love freedom very much. As Greg Shupak, who teaches media studies at the University of Guelph, wrote in a piece for *Jacobin*, "On October 21 2011, 66 bodies were found at the Mahari Hotel, at least 53 of whom were executed by a rebel militia. An undetermined portion of these were Qadhafi loyalists who had been captured along with Qadhafi himself. Those killed at the hotel were shot with rifles and many had their hands tied behind their backs and some can be seen on video being abused before their execution. NATO plainly shares responsibility for these crimes because before NATO bombing commenced, the insurgents were on the verge of defeat and could not have won the war without NATO air cover, arms, money, and diplomatic support."[15]

The anthropologist Maximillian Forte details the crimes of these rebels, and possible NATO war crimes, in a crucial book called *Slouching Towards Sirte*. Citing Forte, Shupak also explains, "The most serious indictment of NATO's rebel allies is their violent treatment of black Libyans and migrant workers from countries in southern Africa. For instance, when Tripoli fell to rebels in August 2011, a reporter for *The Independent* visited a makeshift hospital controlled by the insurgents and found the decomposing bodies of 30 men, many of whom had their hands bound behind their backs and almost all of whom were black."[16]

Maddow's noble war on Libya, fought with all the necessary bells and whistles that international law requires, certainly pales in comparison to her coverage of Iran. At least, in the case of Libya, she left the door open for the possibility that things might not go smoothly, she just never revisited the details that proved they didn't. In the case of Iran, she simply just gets all the facts wrong. On a program that aired in April of 2013, Maddow criticized the US federal holiday system, telling her viewers that even Iran has more federal holidays. Iran! "According to the dictators who run dictatorships," she declared, "there are lots of reasons to stop and reflect and celebrate whatever it is the dictator is telling us to celebrate." She placed the first year of Iran's dictatorship at 1979, seemingly completely unaware of the fact that in 1953, Iranian Prime Minister Mohammad Mossaddegh was removed from office via a CIA-backed coup for the crime of nationalizing his country's oil supply. She then put a graphic up on the screen, full of typos, listing the Iranian holidays. Some major problems arise: it claims the Ayatollahs insist that people celebrate Nowruz, despite the fact they tried to ban it. The graphic also mocks Iran's "Martyrdom of Hazart Fatemesh", presumably assuming that it's a reference to some deceased suicide bomber when, in actuality, the word "Hazart" is an esteemed title. As BBC journalist Shirin Sadeghi wrote in a piece at *Huffington Post,* "The sheer prejudice and outright Saidian orientalism that Maddow exhibited in this 4-minute segment is eerily reminiscent of the Jim Crow days of American broadcasting when 'respectable' journalists and entertainers could get away with insulting an entire race of people, their traditions and their beliefs, without batting an eye. In this case, Maddow has not only insulted Iranians but every Muslim in the world, too. Just imagine the uproar if she took such liberties with any other of the world's major religions."[17]

Ah, but the fun Maddow has with the Islamic Republic of Iran doesn't stop there. In June of 2013, she referenced then-president Mahmoud Ahmadinejad like this: "Mahmoud Ahmadinejad, he's known around the world for defending Iran's pursuit of nuclear weapons." What? Even someone paying minimal attention to current events knows that the opposite is true. Despite the sabre-rattling of a GOP that Maddow consistently mocks, there is no evidence that Ahmandinejad's uranium program was maintained for military reasons. In fact, the former leader of Iran was kind-of-known for regularly declaring that he wasn't trying to develop a nuclear bomb.

Despite the aforementioned facts, the United States has maintained brutal sanctions against the regime, for the alleged cause of stopping their nuclear weapon capability. According to a piece, from *The Guardian,* thousands of Iranians suffering from cancer are now unable to obtain chemotherapy. Additionally, "An estimated 23,000 Iranians with HIV/AIDS have had their access to the drugs they need to keep them alive severely restricted. The society representing the 8,000 Iranians suffering from thalassaemia, an inherited blood disorder, has said its members are beginning to die because of a lack of an essential drug, deferoxamine, used to control the iron content in the blood."[18] These sanctions are similar to the ones carried out against Iraq, under Clinton, that killed thousands of children. When confronted with details of the human toll on *60 Minutes*, then-Secretary of State Madeline Albright, "We think the price is worth it."

Apparently, as far as Iran goes, Maddow believes the price is worth it as well. The people unable to obtain necessary medical supplies would be surprised to discover that, according to Maddow, sanctions have set the stage for progress and ignited important social protests. Interesting! A current petition being circulated by the group Berim, calling on Maddow to discuss the real impact of sanctions currently has 6,515 signatures. It begins, "Rachel Maddow is a fantastic journalist, but last week my jaw dropped when she said that international sanctions had caused the Iranian people to fight for change. That's just wrong. In 2009 millions of ordinary Iranians fought for change, some even lost their lives standing up for their beliefs. That happened well before President Obama escalated sanctions."

This is all from a journalist who believes herself to be completely objective. When *Reason's* Nick Gillespie confronted Maddow about her partisanship during an episode of Bill Maher's show, pointing out that she would always take the side of Democrat, she shot back, "No, I won't. You don't even know me."

"I've seen your show," responded Gillespie.

IN THE JEEP:
IMPERIALISM, ISRAEL AND MSNBC

It's very possible that everything you need to know about the young *Washington Post* columnist and MSNBC contributor Ezra Klein, can be deduced from the opening line of a *New Republic* profile on him: "The first time I interviewed Ezra Klein, the 28-year-old prince of D.C. media, he brought me a sandwich: prosciutto on a poppy-seed baguette."[19]

Nonetheless, I am going to proceed anyway. Ezra Klein has established himself as a hospitable prop of Beltway scenery despite the fact he may, or may not be, an android. As Bhaskar Sunkara wrote in a piece about his brand of wonkery "At some point, Klein and company stopped being liberals. They even stopped being human. The singularity—a technological superintelligence—was upon us. The wonks had become robots, ready to force enlightenment down our partisan throats." He's referring to a particular strain of post-political pundit, reflexively liberal on social issues yet committed to nothing beyond incrementalism economically, that began gaining favor during the dark days of Bush. Klein's bio, prior to becoming an MSNBC contributor, looks exactly how you would expect it to: he worked on Howard Dean's overestimated Presidential campaign, interned for the *Washington Monthly*, and started his own blog before being picked up to write for the *American Prospect.* Despite his embrace of Dean, Klein supported the overthrow of Saddam Hussein, falling in line with many prominent liberal interventionists of the time.

Recently, amidst somber reflections on the attack's ten-year anniversary, Klein issued a mea culpa for his warmongering. He cited his youthful embrace of a terrible military invasion as, "an analytical failure." One wonders what kind of computer program generates such an apology, but I digress. Klein wrote, "It wasn't worth doing precisely because the odds were high that we couldn't do it 'right."

The terminology used here is worth a closer examination. Klein's concession may lack emotion, but it also assumes a telling relation between journalist and government. As the political theorist Corey Robin wrote, in response to Klein's apology, "Klein doesn't think a state invaded another state; he thinks 'we' went to war. He identifies with the state. Whether he's supporting or dissenting from a policy, he sees himself as part of it. He sees himself on the jeeps with the troops. That's why his calls for skepticism, for not taking things on authority, ring so hollow. In the end, he's on the team. Or the jeep."

Notable, and egregious, examples of jeep riding define the MSNBC experience. Let's start with Touré, a former hip-hop journalist who promised to stop writing about the culture after 2Pac and Biggie were murdered. He lied about that, returning to rap coverage, writing a popular book about race, and eventually becoming a co-host of MSNBC's *The Cycle.* He also accomplished the amazing feat of generating sympathy for the ludicrous Piers Morgan, after he went on the British talk show host's program to discuss the tragic death of Trayvon Martin. Touré began by calling Morgan "part of the problem", for the crime of having interviewed, Trayvon's killer, George Zimmerman. He then told Morgan, "Do you know that in the hallways of NBC we were laughing at you today? We wouldn't even take 'em–standards of practices at NBC wouldn't even let them through the door." "Maybe that goes in England," reasoned Touré sarcastically, as he continued to berate Morgan for the crime of tepid journalism.

Trayvon Martin was, of course, only 17 years old when he was fatally shot by George Zimmerman, his whole life ahead of him. Months before Martin's murder, a teenager named Abdulrahman al-Awlaki was killed by an American drone strike in Yemen. He had ran away from home in an effort to find his father, Anwar al-Awlaki, another US citizen assassinated by his own government. The details of Anwar al-Awlaki's radicalization, and ultimate, demise are detailed in Jeremy Scahill's *Dirty Wars*. It's a disturbing, yet illuminating, story that reads like a spy-novel. The US allegedly targeted al-Anwar because they believed he was directly connected to terrorist activity. Although the details of this allegation are murkier than the Obama administration lets on, and he was entitled to a trial nonetheless, we know that Anwar was praising attacks on Americans via YouTube at time of his murder.

However, no one from the administration has ever even pretended that his 16-year-old son, who had his face blown off while sitting in an outdoor café, had any connection to terrorism at all. As Scahill has consistently tried to tell the American people, he was just a goofy, carefree kid with a Facebook who lived with his grandfather and loved hanging out with his friends. When questioned about the targeted killing of Abdulrahman, which the administration has barely ever even acknowledged, Robert Gibbs (who went on to become a pundit on MSNBC after his stint as White House Press Secretary) suggested the teenager would still be alive if he "had a better father." Around the same time as Gibbs's heartless aside, Touré raised a few eyebrows by arguing that President Obama had the right to assassinate an American citizen, even if he was a completely innocent teenager. In fact, during an MSNBC panel discussing drone strikes, Touré seemed completely unaware that Abdulrahman, had ever even existed: "What do you mean a 16-year old who is killed? I'm not talking about civilians", he declared, when the subject came up. After fellow panelists, liberal Steve Kornacki and conservative S.E. Cupp, explained to Touré who Abdulrahman Al-Awlaki was, he shrugged, "If people are working against America, then they need to die."

Touré's hypocrisy is chilling. He, rightly, demands more rigorous analysis of Trayvon Martin's senseless death, but brushes off the equally disturbing case of Abdulrahman al-Awlaki. Where is the pushback, which Touré demands of journalists like Piers Morgan, covering the Trayvon Martin case, on the Obama administration's morally reprehensible justifications for death and destruction? The political theorist Falguni Sheth brilliantly took Touré to task for failing to connect the dots between the two deaths, "There is a certain nativist, if not xenophobic, consistency on Touré's part. Rightfully insisting on paying attention to the racist context surrounding Martin's death, he nevertheless challenges Morgan's attitudes on the grounds that Morgan is not "from here." For all of Touré's understanding about the racial context of unfair murders, he appears to be ignorant of and indifferent to the fact that a young Muslim (American) boy was killed by a drone under the auspices of the POTUS. We see a similar nativism in Touré's sentiments about restricting due process to "Americans"—even after he learns that Abdulrahman Al-Awlaki IS American."[20]

After his causal, seemingly confused, comments on the drone strike, Touré seemed to double-down on his position, taking on Twitter critics and insisting that civilians weren't being targeted. After someone informed him that civilians were, in fact, being killed, telling him about Abdulrahman's killing once again, Touré sarcastically shot back, "A military failing?" A government purposely targeting a teenager for no apparent reason, then refusing to even apologize for it, strikes me as a pretty broad definition of failure, but Touré remained strident in his support of assassination.

By the next time the topic came up on his program, Touré had, evidently, learned a few things about these assassinations; he learned they actually occurred, for starters. When Jeremy Scahill, a guest on the show, made an offhand comment about how the Obama administration should have presented evidence against Anwar al-Awlaki in a court of law, Touré was ready to jump to the President's defense, armed with some recently obtained facts on the subject.

Touré: They did present evidence, Jeremy; you know that, [in] in a Yemeni court

Scahill: What's the evidence? [What] what was the evidence, Touré?

Touré: Well, [I mean,] I don't have it here in front of me, but he was convicted in, he was convicted in, he was convicted in a Yemeni court.

Scahill: Would you want to be prosecuted in a Yemeni court? [Let me ask you, (?)] Would you want to be prosecuted in a Yemeni court? This is a country that set up a tribunal to prosecute journalists for crimes against the dictator. If you're holding up the Yemeni justice system as a place where you think an American citizen's going to get a fair trial, then I would invite you to go to Yemen and start jaywalking and see what kind of treatment you're going to get in those courts 'cause you can't have it both ways, man—if you want to act like Yemen's courts are legitimate, you better act like they're legitimate when they put political prisoners in there or they put people in there for crimes against a dictatorship, so [don't] don't come at me with something about a Yemeni court, this is an American citizen, who should have had access to due process before he was sentenced to death by the constitutional law professor president.

Touré never got around to answering whether he would like to be tried in a Yemeni court. In the end, his failure to perceive the link between Trayvon Martin and Abdulrahman al-Awlaki is highlighted, all the more, by critics who actually did. "Our righteous indignation and anger over the Trayvon Martin murder has to stretch beyond our community to consider a global humanity – and especially the nonwhite victims of US militarism and racism," wrote *Black Agenda Reporter's* Jemima Pierre. "We must pause and reflect on the injustice of the US government's extrajudicial assassinations, and the fact that the Obama administration has claimed the right to kill people in multiple countries around the world whenever it wants."

In Touré 's defense, he did allow Scahill to speak, which is more than can be said for Martin Bashir, who didn't even let, GOP strategist, Trey Hardin finish a sentence before cutting him off. Bashir, who gained fame after his series of interviews with the late Michael Jackson, hosts a program, named after him, on MSNBC. During the summer of 2012, Bashir hosted a debate on the Obama administration's support of government leaks when they're to their advantage, an important subject that should surpass the limitations of partisanship. After playing a clip of Joint Chiefs Chairman General Martin Dempsey, arguing that military members should always be apolitical, Bashir threw it over to the Republican. Hardin began, or tried to begin, by pointing out that Dempsey's comments shouldn't be that surprising, as he works for the President. That was too much for Colonel Bashir, who booted Hardin right away, "I'm sorry, I cannot allow you to cast such a contemptuous aspersion against a senior military officer by demeaning his service to this country. Will you please take that comment back? ... Sir, he serves the United States of America."

"These are the prohibited thought crimes as decreed by a 'journalist' on a progressive cable network," wrote Glenn Greenwald. "All that because Hardin had the temerity merely to point out that as a direct subordinate of Obama's who works with him on a daily basis, Dempsey has an interest in defending him from political attacks – that he's not some unimpeachable Oracle of Truth before whose very pronouncements we must all bow. Not even the Spanish Inquisition entailed such delicate, hair-trigger recriminations for blasphemy as the one that set off this MSNBC host yesterday on his little patriotism enforcement crusade."[21]

The proverbial jeeps are not always adorned with the decals of the domestic military, but sometimes emblazoned with the markings of client states. The ultimate example of such a state is, of course, Israel; a country which has, essentially, been used as a satellite by the United States since 1967, after it dealt a heavy blow to Arab secular nationalism by destroying Egypt in the Six-Day War. The Nixon administration recognized Israel to be "one of the cops on the beat", a force that could effectively stomp out any further bursts of independence that might pop in the region. For its efforts, Israel is given over $3 billion in taxpayer money every year and allowed to continue its brutal occupation of Palestinian territories.

Nearly every one of these crucial facts was omitted from Rachel Maddow's explanation of the Israeli-Palestinian conflict, which was delivered to her television audience in 2009, after Israel launched a fresh round of attacks against Gaza, "Jewish state, right smack-dab in the middle of the Arab world. Surrounded on all sides by Arab nations, many of who do not recognize Israel's right to exist. Israel was, in a sense, conceived by war. A day after it declared its independence in May, 1948, it was attacked by five neighboring countries, Egypt, Jordan, Syria, Lebanon, and Iraq. What followed were decades of endless wars, fought on and near Israeli soil. A war with Egypt in 1956, another with Egypt and Jordan and Syria in 1967, another with Egypt and Syria in 1973, one with Lebanon in 1982, and so on, and so on, and so on."

And on and on. This assessment, regularly pumped out by media members, suggests that the two sides are prone to violence and, simply, locked into some primitive battle that has been handed down for generations. The fact that Israeli violence is paid for by the United States, and the fact that much of it could be ended in an instant if the American government wanted it to, is never even approached. The "Peace Process" itself has developed into an industry; a complicated puzzle that our best minds have been attempting to solve for years. Of course, the key to cracking the riddle is, probably, somehow connected to the $67 billion that American taxpayers have shelled out to Israel since they began occupying the West Bank.

This all serves as necessary preface for our next subject: Adam Serwer, a journalist hired by MSNBC during the spring of 2013. New to the game, the details of his jeep riding can only be extracted by carefully combing the Internet. One can start by checking out a blog post about a soccer game. Commenting on the ceremony preceding a woman's USA match, journalist Charles Davis blogged that, "No other country on Earth, barring perhaps North Korea, worships its military in such a prevalent, mindless and such seemingly oblivious fashion as the good 'ol USA." This comment drew ire from Serwer, a *Mother Jones* blogger who was hired by MSNBC in May of 2013. He told Davis, "We should support service members unconditionally because their service is unconditional, and I have yet to hear a rational argument for why allowing service members to disregard civilian authority over the military is a good idea, which is essentially what calling for civil disobedience by service members is...The whole point of civilian control is to ensure that the people with guns don't get to do whatever they want, that the power given them can only be used with the consent of the political branches, elected by the people. And if you don't think that power is being used properly, [then] you can change that through the political process."[22]

Davis responded on his blog, "But no one's arguing, of course, that soldiers should merely do whatever they feel. The argument, at least as I have made it, is that killing people is wrong, except in instances of absolute self-defense, no matter what politician or politically appointed court sanctions it. Now, abiding by one's conscience is typically consistent with the whole not murdering people thing — poor foreigner or not — but where it differs, it's subservient to that latter, foundational principal of any truly civilized society. Again, the argument is that people ought to defy orders to kill — and ostracize, rather than worship, the institutions tasked with carrying out the state-sponsored carnage — not that they should kill more people if they feel like it. And instead of wading through a corrupt political process designed to thwart change and serve the needs of the powerful, the legitimacy of which Serwer asserts but does not bother to demonstrate, it's the responsibility of all human beings with a capacity for moral thought, be they uniformed or not, to reject blind obedience authority and the 'legal' facade it provides to immoral acts. The idea that only the political process is an acceptable means of challenging injustice treats the average person as but an unthinking cog in the machinery of the state, bound to abide by whatever 'lawful' edicts their rulers issue, a worldview that does not allow for principled civil disobedience. We, soldier and citizen, are not entitled to determine what's right and wrong, whether it be a preemptive war or, say, the institution of slavery — that's left to legislatures."

This thoughtful response prompted the following comeback from Serwer: "We do have some job openings, but nothing quite as prestigious as writing for Code Pink, I'm sad to say."

Serwer has demonstrated a similarly disparaging tone towards Max Blumenthal, an award-winning journalist who has documented the rise of Israeli racism over the last few years. After Blumenthal wrote a piece, during the height of the Occupy movement, about American police adopting Israeli military tactics, he was attacked by, *Atlantic* staff writer, Jeffrey Goldberg, a former IDF prison guard, consistent West Bank occupation shill, and current Iran attack enthusiast, best known for regurgitating the Bush administration's Iraq War propaganda in the pages of the *New Yorker*, and imagining an operative connection between Saddam Hussein and Al-Qaeda.

Goldberg attacked Blumenthal for misquoting Karen Greenberg, the director of the Fordham School of Law's Center on National Security, in his piece. In the story, Blumenthal quotes Greenberg telling him, "After 9/11 we reached out to the Israelis on many fronts and one of those fronts was torture. The training in Iraq and Afghanistan on torture was Israeli training. There's been a huge downside to taking our cue from the Israelis and now we're going to spread that into the fabric of everyday American life? It's counter-terrorism creep. And it's exactly what you could have predicted would have happened."[23]

Goldberg contacted Greenberg about the quote and she, apparently, claimed to have never made such a statement. Goldberg called on Blumenthal to issue a correction, but rather than back down, Blumenthal stood up to Goldberg's infamous thuggery, declaring, "I am not sure why Greenberg would deny the statement she made to me on the record unless she was intimidated by Goldberg and the pro-Israel forces he represents. But the salient fact is that I did quote her accurately, word for word, and I stand by my reporting." He later added, "Greenberg's statement to me did not come out of the blue: A book she co-authored with Joshua Dratel, "The Road to Abu Ghraib," contains a lengthy section on Israeli court rulings authorizing torture and torture techniques refined by the Shin Bet. In a subsequent article, Greenberg and Dratel proposed questions for Donald Rumsfeld about torture. Here is one: 'Did your discussions of torture involve consulting experts in Israel..?'"

Out of nowhere, Serwer jumped into the fray, calling Greenberg and asking her to clarify the situation, knowing full well that she had already denied making the comments. At the time, Serwer was blogging for *Mother Jones*, and he wrote up a short post attacking Blumenthal on the magazine's website. However, in a series of emails about the subject, with labor writer Mike Elk, Serwer essentially admitted that Blumenthal may have been quoting Greenberg correctly, he was really just miffed about this piece, "Greenberg is a frequent source of mine. She felt misquoted/ taken out of context, and she doesn't have the knowledge to back up the claim Max attributed to her. Even if Max quoted her words accurately, the underlying claim that Israeli interrogators trained the US in torture isn't proven. I have no idea if it's false or not, but it's not proven, because (a) Max didn't prove it and (b) the person he quoted to substantiate the claim says she doesn't know if it's true."

What? Serwer accuses a journalist of purposely misquoting a source, a grave accusation to level at a reporter, and then admits he's not even sure that Blumenthal misquoted her? If Serwer had a problem with the content of Blumenthal's piece, then why didn't he simply compose a post arguing against its merits? Why jump in bed with an individual like Goldberg and question the very integrity of the author? As Mark Ames wrote of the debacle, "Is *Mother Jones* now in the business of smearing journalism that dares to investigate the ties between U.S. police departments responsible for violently crushing the Occupy protests, and Israeli occupation forces that violently repress Palestinians? What are the venerable labor-left magazine's editorial guidelines and ethical standards?" The same as MSNBC's apparently, but I digress.

Search the Internet long, and hard, enough and come across an alternative persona for Serwer: a blogger who goes by the alias "dnA." It's a moniker that Serwer has admitted being behind and, it doesn't take much effort to find a piece by dnA attacking Blumenthal. Under this formerly-anonymous pseudonym, Serwer went after Blumenthal's criticism of *New York Times* columnist Frank Rich, after Rich had written a column imagining that the end of American racism was on the horizon. Written during the cutthroat Democratic primary between Clinton and Obama, Serwer seemed to be under the impression that, because his father was an advisor to former President Bill Clinton, Blumenthal's critique of Rich must stem from some kind of pro-Hillary, anti-Obama position. In fact, in the original draft of the post, he incorrectly cites Max, not his father, as having worked for the Clinton's.

So why is Serwer consistently attacking Blumenthal, one of the Israeli Occupation's harshest critics? Liberal supporters of Israel often brandish their progressive credentials before launching an attack. For instance, in Serwer's anti-Blumenthal post, he points out, "In case it's not clear, I don't aspire to spend my professional life trying to silence Israel's critics and Israel has plenty of its own issues with torture, human rights, and the rule of law." The implication here is that, if Serwer is attacking a critic of Israel, there must be some validity to his position, as he does not typically defend Israel.

In a piece for the *Washington Post*, Serwer repped Obama's call for a peace deal and wrote that, "For too long, the term 'pro-Israel' in the American political context been used to describe only those who minimize the suffering of Palestinians and actively enable the Israeli right's attempt to bring the peace process to a halt, even as they offer rhetorical support for the idea of a two state solution. But political changes in the Middle East and demographic changes in the region have created a shrinking window of time for Israel to seek a resolution to the conflict on terms favorable to its long-term survival."[24]

Serwer has the acceptable stances on Israel mapped out: on one side is the right-wing Israeli government, not shy about their soft-spot for ethnic cleansing and, on the other side, is Team Obama, who pays lip service to the Palestinian cause while acknowledging that Israel faces an existential threat. Serwer, and Obama, realize the "peril the country faces, both as a Jewish state and a democracy." I'm not sure if Serwer has ever even been to Israel, but he has evidently established such a strong connection to the country that he feels a loyalty to it. "There's nothing actually wrong with having divided loyalties—if that means that being Jewish means that Israel matters more to you than America," Serwer wrote in a piece for *The Root*. "This is part of the game in a nation made up of immigrants—the politics of affiliated nations matter. It's part of the double standard shouldered by ethnic and religious minorities that such behavior is seen as somehow sinister. I'll cop to caring about Israel more because I'm Jewish—but that doesn't mean I'll evaluate its actions uncritically out of blind loyalty. In fact, in most cases it's precisely because liberal Jewish bloggers care about Israel that they're critical of its actions: They see Israel's behavior in the region, particularly its treatment of the Palestinians, as harming Israel's long-term interests."[25]

Back on planet Earth, Serwer's narrative falls apart immediately. Obama, and the liberal bloggers who have supported him on this issue, might view the President as some sort of necessary bulwark against Israel's right-wing turn, but his administration has been a complete failure in this regard. Looking back on those impassioned days of the 2008 campaign, and the rhetoric that defined the subject, now seems especially comical; it wasn't so long ago that the GOP constructed an operative connection between Obama and, the late, great advocate for Palestinian self-determination, Edward Said. His Middle East policy has proven these concerns utterly hilarious. In fact, it would not be a very challenging task to prove that he has, somehow, been even worse than his predecessor on the issue. As Josh Ruebner, founder of Jews for Peace in

Palestine and Israel, writes, "Under the Obama administration, the White House and Congress worked hand in glove to elevate US-Israel military ties to unprecedented levels in at least three ways. First, Obama requested and Congress appropriated the record-breaking levels of military aid to Israel, which have now plateaued at $3.1 billion annually, envisioned in the 2007 MOU. Second, in addition to this munificent military aid, Obama requested and Congress appropriated ever-increasing levels of money for the joint research and development of various anti-missile programs, which amounted to more than $1 billion during Obama's first term. These supposedly 'defensive' weapons drastically changed Israel's strategic thinking, making it virtually cost-free for it to go on the offensive against Palestinians while effectively protecting its own civilian populations from retaliatory fire. The deployment of these Iron Dome batteries, designed to knock down short-range projectiles, therefore increases, rather than lessens, the likelihood of another major conflagration on the scale of Operation Cast Lead. Third, joint US-Israel military exercises and US prepositioning of war material in Israel also expanded to unprecedented degrees during the Obama administration."[26]

There is, also, a much deeper question that needs to be asked here, a question which cuts to the core of Serwer's brand of liberal Zionism: why does he believe Israel must continue to be maintained as a Jewish state, as opposed to a state in which all religions and ethnicities are accepted? The crisis of contemporary Israeli society transcends the occupation and, additionally, takes form in the shape of attacks against the country's African population. In May of 2012, a thousand Israelis ran through the streets, smashing the windows of African-run businesses and physically assaulting non-whites. These antics were condoned by Israeli lawmakers like Miri Regev, who referred to African migrants as "a cancer in the body" of Israel. The riot showcased a prevalent racial outlook. As David Sheen wrote, in an article marking the event's anniversary, "For African asylum seekers who haven't been swept off the streets into incarceration, humiliation and exploitation are the norm. Public buildings refuse them admittance and force them to wait for service outside in the cold or in dismal underground parking lots. Many Africans are afraid to even jaywalk across the street, petrified of being picked up for even the slightest infraction and being sent to jail indefinitely without trial. Israeli citizens know full well that

African asylum seekers' rights and freedoms are precarious and subject to summary revocation. "[27]

If these actions, along with the daily injustice of occupied Palestine, are what it takes to keep Israel sufficiently Jewish, then one wonders if liberal Zionists like Serwer believe the end justifies the means. The object of Serwer's scorn, Max Blumenthal, wrote an entire book examining these very points, *Goliath: Life and Loathing in Greater Israel.* The text was dismissed and/or attacked in all the predictable venues, (including *The Nation*, where columnist, and former MSNBC.com contributor, Eric Alterman declared that any discussion of the book shamed the pages of the venerated liberal magazine), but it contains a scene which diagnoses the deficiencies in Serwer's stance perfectly. In one scene, Blumenthal interviews the heralded novelist David Grossman, long-viewed as a principled liberal advocating for peace in the region. When Blumenthal asks Grossman why Israel can't shift, from an exclusively Jewish state, to a multiethnic democracy, Grossman tells him, "For two thousand years we have been kept out, we have been excluded. And so for our whole history we were outsiders. Because of Zionism, we finally have the chance to be insiders."[28]

Blumenthal then tells Grossman that his father was, in fact, an insider, having worked as an aide for the Clinton administration. He tells him that he worked alongside many other Jewish people and that, in some ways, he thought of himself as an insider. Such a statement could easily be applied to Serwer as well, whose father was a counselor at the Department of State and a Deputy Chief of Mission and chargé d'affaires at the U.S. Embassy in Rome. Blumenthal writes that, after confronted with the information about his dad, "[Grossman] looked at me with a quizzical look. Very few Israelis understand American Jews as Americans but instead as belonging to the Diaspora. But very few American Jews think of themselves that way, especially in my generation, and that, too, is something very few Israelis grasp. Grossman's silence made me uncomfortable, as though I had behaved with impudence, and I quickly shifted the subject from philosophy to politics. Before long, we said goodbye, parting cordially, but not warmly. On my way out of the café, Grossman, apparently wishing to preserve his privacy, requested that I throw my record of his phone number away."

****

In his book, *Killer Politics: How Big Money and Bad Politics Are Destroying the Great American Middle Class*, MSNBC's Ed Schultz quotes Barack Obama's Nobel Peace Prize speech before opining, "I do not believe that preemptive war with Iraq was justified. I think it was a blunder that set a dangerous modern-day precedent for preemptive war and seriously damaged U.S. credibility around the world-something only time and credible action in the future can mitigate. History alone knows how this war will play out. What we can be certain about is that Bush's Iraq folly placed a tremendous financial burden on the nation that has critically weakened us both militarily and financially."

The word *blunder* is defined as "a gross, stupid, or careless mistake." The noun assumes a level of noble intent, which Schultz bestows upon the same Bush administration he railed against each night. Despite disagreeing adamantly with Bush's decision to go to war, Schultz views the invasion of a Middle Eastern country, and a subsequent occupation defined by torture and death, as a "folly." a tactical mistake made by a flawed leader. Schultz's view of Iraq is not dissimilar to the Vietnam-era liberals, who criticized the war effort

On an episode of *Real Time With Bill Maher*, after Maher criticized an Obama speech on the future of Afghanistan, Schultz leapt to his defense, "The bottom line here is: he didn't get us in there, he's trying to get us out." While interviewing Representative Alan Grayson on his own show, Schultz asked if Barack Obama could have, plausibly, been elected if he had talked about increasing troops in Afghanistan during his campaign, the implication being that Obama lied about his desire to increase the troop-size to get elected and, then, save Afghanistan by sticking more soldiers there.

But Barack Obama *did* talk about increasing troop levels in Afghanistan during his campaign. In fact, he talked about it quite a bit. In a *Slate* essay by the late War on Terror enthusiast, Christopher Hitchens titled, "Pakistan is the Problem", Hitchens endorsed Obama precisely because he was the more hawkish candidate, "Sen. Barack Obama has, if anything, been the more militant of the two presidential candidates in stressing the danger here and the need to act without too much sentiment about our so-called Islamabad ally." After a decade of being wrong about so very much, Hitchens's prognostication of the Obama administration turned out to be completely accurate: "American liberals can't quite face the fact that if their man does win in November, and if he has meant a single serious word he's ever said, it means more war, and more bitter and protracted war at that—not less."[29]

Hitchens wasn't the only Obama supporter that should have drawn contemplation from the candidate's ebullient fans. The Senator from Illinois was also backed by torture-defender Alan Dershowitz and Iraq War architect Colin Powell. These endorsements generated no concern from voters who perceived Obama as a welcomed departure from Bush's policy. But they also weren't examined by MSNBC in any capacity, beyond their proof that Obama was a special kind of politician with the ability to rise above partisan disagreements. That's how they roll.

CHRIS HAYES:
The Exception and the Rule

"All the animals, the plants, the minerals, even other kinds of men, are being broken and reassembled every day, to preserve an elite few, who are the loudest to theorize on freedom, but the least free of all."

-Thomas Pynchon, *Gravity's Rainbow*

Even the most robust of MSNBC criticisms often includes a seemingly crucial disclaimer. That warning generally involves Christopher Hayes, Editor-at-Large at *The Nation* magazine, and host of his own nightly show on MSNBC, *All In with Chris Hayes*, formerly a weekend program called *Up With Chris Hayes*. Hayes's own personal world is the paradigm of stereotypical liberalism. His mother works for the NYC Department of Education, he attended Hunter College High School and Brown University. His brother Luke worked on Obama's 2012 reelection campaign and his wife, Kate Shaw, is former associate counsel to President Obama. He became a consistent staple at MSNBC after filling in for Maddow and credits her with launching his television career. Maddow believes Hayes to be, "the young left's most erudite and urgent interpreter."

The instinctual defense of Hayes' commentary is birthed out of the belief that he stands in as what passes as the far-left in today's media climate, for better or worse. Noam Chomsky used to identify the *New*

York Times' Anthony Lewis as the litmus test for how radical journalists could get within the mainstream. This quick rule of thumb dictated that, anything to the left of an Anthony Lewis column would be a challenge to get by an editor. The prevailing belief is that Hayes now occupies that spot. His show is frequently worth watching and doesn't fall back on the predictable level of snark that defines the network's other programming. He frequently invites guests not normally interviewed by the American media; not just critical national security journalists like Jeremy Scahill and the late Michael Hastings, but striking Wal-Mart workers and Occupy Wall Street protesters. After Israel's most recent attack on Gaza, Hayes had more than one Palestinian on his panel, a virtually unprecedented move for a rabidly pro-Israel media.

This is all frequently refreshing, as far as it goes, but a closer examination of Hayes' politics tells us a great deal about contemporary liberalism's restrictions and deficiencies. We start with Hayes' book, finished shortly before the original incarnation of his show kicked off, *Twilight of the Elites: America After Meritocracy.* It's a well-written analysis of our culture's flaws and inequalities, but provides virtually nothing beyond banal center-left solutions. Our elites have failed us, argues Chris Hayes, and who would dare argue with him after the last decade of American disaster? However, his response to this seems like a parody of contemporary liberalism's long list of failures.[30]

"The argument I make in the book, and it's a tentative argument, but I do think there is a potential for a radicalized upper-middle class," Hayes explained in an interview with *Jacobin.* "We already see that, it's just a question of how that gets channeled. Everything about the Netroots, the anti-war, anti-Bush sentiment [the Tea Party is also cited in the book]. One of the interesting things about the way our certain kind of fractal inequality has manifested, the people who see it the most, have the closest proximity to it, say, the top 2 to the top 20 percent: 'I went to law school with Joe and I have some job at a firm and I'm doing alright, but he went into a hedge fund and is making $10 million.'"

Huh? For starters, Hayes' implicit dismissal of the working-class is predicated on the belief that they no longer hold any political power. Whether that's true is open for debate, but the suggestion that they have to be led forward through a more humane ruling-class completely disregards potential solutions that put working people first. That is to say, it disregards the very solutions, and visions, that defined the left for years. Hayes's failure to recognize any answer that transcends Neoliberalism says a great deal about how he perceives the engine of social change, but the restrictions of his approach seem completely lost on him. For instance, during that same interview with *Jacobin,* he cites Latin America as a blueprint for success, explaining, "The basic story of Latin America: 10 to 20 years of IMF imposed austerity and structural adjustment, that created terrible crisis, terrible poverty, and terrible inequality which provoked a backlash across the continent. Left and center-left leaders were voted in who had mandates and political coalitions in which inequality was explicitly part of their agenda and then implemented policies that were egalitarian."

This assessment sounds great, but the suggestion that leaders were simply voted in with mandates, obscures an important dynamic of recent revolutions in the area. In the United States, leaders are elected with political mandates and the people simply hope that they implement them. In Latin America, leaders frequently emerged *from* the people, from the very classes that Hayes's analysis writes off. George Ciccariello-Maher, Assistant Professor of Political Science at Drexel University, wrote an entire book about how the process occurred in Venezuela, aptly titled, *We Created Chavez: A People's History of the Venezuelan Revolution.* As Joe Emersberger writes, in his review of the book, "The 1980s brought a devastating and very prolonged economic collapse (largely due to falling oil prices) and increased government violence against those who protested, however legally, for relief. The urban poor, independent of armed rebels who sought to lead them, began to organize themselves for self-help and armed self-defense in the 1970s. These groups became more important as conditions worsened in the 1980s. Responding to immediate community concerns, they became preoccupied with eradicating the drug trade in their neighborhoods which pitted them against both drug traffickers and police. The emergence of these groups marked the beginning of the popular militia movement that would partially characterize the Chavez government years later."[31]

This kind of stuff is hardly what Hayes has in mind. As Freddie Deboer wrote, in an essay on the book, "Hayes looks out at a burning house and with true moral conviction and unsparing vision, describes it. He then proposes solutions that amount to washing the windows while the building is engulfed in flames...his prescriptions for solving the massive problems he identifies in the book are the typical incrementalism that has constrained the American left for over 30 years...All Karl Marx in description, all Tom Daschle in prescription."[32]

Yes, Hayes has a movement in mind: "One that marshals insurrectionist sentiment without succumbing to nihilism and manic, paranoid distrust. One that avoids the dark seduction of everything-is-broken-ism. One that leverages the deep skepticism of elites into a proactive, constructive vision of moral, equitable, and connected social order." While keeping those technocratic caveats in mind, ponder the fact that Hayes once wrote, "I'm not sure what is in me, or our culture, or the generational attitudes of post-baby booms progressives, but I have a visceral cringe reaction to a lot of protest politics."

You'd think this variation of flawed liberalism would fit in perfectly at MSNBC, but, in May of 2012, Hayes actually went too far, surpassing the afforded lines of respectable discourse, and kicking up something resembling a controversy. Hosting a panel convened to talk about the subject of Memorial Day, Hayes questioned whether all dead American soldiers were, in fact, heroes. "It is very difficult to talk about the war dead and the fallen without invoking valor, without invoking the word hero. Why do I feel so uncomfortable about the word hero?" Hayes asked. "I feel uncomfortable with the word hero because it seems to me that it is so rhetorically proximate to justifications for more war. And I obviously don't want to desecrate or disrespect the memory of anyone that has fallen. Obviously there are individual circumstances in which there is tremendous heroism. You know, hail of gunfire, rescuing fellow soldiers, things like that. But it seems to me that we marshal this word in a way that's problematic, but maybe I'm wrong about that."

This offhand, commonsensical observation was a truly compelling moment of television. Hayes was challenging the language that we use to justify unjust wars. For years, liberals had been trotting out evasive platitudes like, "I don't support the war, but I support the troops." Hayes had, almost accidentally, made a brilliant and thought-provoking point. He was encouraging a dialogue to open up regarding our acceptance of war as a way of life. It's the idea that had pissed off Adam Serwer and alluded Rachel Maddow. He wasn't talking about a specific war, he was saying something very profound about our culture.

One could see the conservative backlash mounting as soon as Hayes finished the sentence. "Chris Hayes' recent remarks on MSNBC regarding our fallen service members are reprehensible and disgusting," declared National Commander of Veterans of Foreign Wars, Richard DeNoyer, and his sentiment set the tone. Ann Coulter even took to Twitter to make a crack about Hayes wearing tampons.

However, the reverberations of Hayes' analysis were felt far beyond the parameters of the right-wing talk machine. Hayes had made a grave mistake, going beyond the kind of allotted military waste critiques, that his colleague Maddow was known for, and questioning the very philosophies that fuel the United States' devotion to perpetual war. Hayes had, inadvertently, hit the third rail of American discourse. He tried to explain himself, urging critics to go back and watch what he actually said, but it was too late. Eventually, he had to issue an apology on his blog and on his program, which was painful to watch.

"Who was I to say who is and isn't a hero?" he asked rhetorically. "It hardly seems like it's a designation that is mine to deny or even to confer." He continued, "We have a society that on the one hand has become comfortable with war and on the other hand wants to distance itself from it as much as possible, to outsource it to contractors, to robots and to the 2.3 million volunteer men and women who have been asked to serve for longer durations than at any time in recent history. Our political culture sometimes seems engineered entirely to make us hate each other. What we're trying to do here on this show, and obviously we don't always succeed, is to talk about sometimes quite sensitive topics in good faith … we tried to do that last week, but I fell short in a crucial moment."

But did Hayes really fall short? Progressives often criticize the American military, for wasting a lot of money or being involved in various clandestine operations and, sure, that's important, but any true attempt to pry us from the grip of, what Eisenhower referred to as, the Military-Industrial Complex, will require an existential reckoning, not just an economic one. It was Martin Luther King, someone frequently cited by liberals as the iconic symbol of admirable struggle, who said, "A true revolution of values will lay hands on the world order and say of war: 'This way of settling differences is not just.' This business of burning human beings with napalm, of filling our nation's homes with orphans and widows, of injecting poisonous drugs of hate into veins of people normally humane, of sending men home from dark and bloody battlefields physically handicapped and psychologically deranged, cannot be reconciled with wisdom, justice and love. A nation that continues year after year to spend more money on military defense than on programs of social uplift is approaching spiritual death."

A "revolution of values" would, no doubt, take into account that all recent American military excursions have been wars of aggression, waged against countries for the purpose of geopolitical control. If every soldier storming into Afghanistan or Iraq is a hero, merely by extension of being American, then logic dictates, soldiers on the opposing side should be viewed as heroes, by their fellow citizens. Unless of course, it's believed that our soldiers' heroic qualities are predetermined, which would open an entirely new, doubly problematic, can of worms. These are kinds of questions we must ask, and the kinds of discussions we must have, if we ever hope to live in a country that doesn't possess an aggressive, and murderous, foreign policy. If a journalist, like Hayes, doesn't believe it's his place to broach these topics, then whose job does he think it should be? At present, it's the very elite that he criticizes who maintain the privilege. The fallout surrounding Hayes was reminiscent of the controversy that engulfed comedian Bill Maher, after he made an infamous offhand comment in the wake of 9/11. Recall that Maher's indiscretion wasn't a criticism of the war in Afghanistan, which the liberal talk-show host enthusiastically backed, but an assessment of, the American way, of dropping bombs as cowardly when compared to the violence of suicide-bombers.

Hayes has never touched the third-rail since. In fact, my own impression is that, ever since that fateful Memorial Day weekend, he has gone the way of Ezra Klein. Who, but a robot, would come up with this line:

"There is a level at which coverage of Republican intransigence produces a visceral effect in the audience that is in some ways less conflicted and more pleasurable than critical coverage of President Obama. It just produces a different effect in the viewer"?[33]

His apparent conversion to electro-mechanical machine has made following Hayes on Twitter a tremendously confounding experience. You are never quite sure what Chris Hayes will see but, more often than not, it is not what you are seeing. In fact, it's often something no one else seems to be seeing.

In May of 2013, Code Pink activist Medea Benjamin interrupted an Obama speech, on drones, asking the President about civilian deaths. The administration has faced sharp criticism, and international condemnation, for its drone program, an operation that has killed thousands of civilians and produced vast amounts of anti-American blowback. "Will you tell the Muslim people their lives are as precious as our lives?" Benjamin yelled at Obama. "Can you take the drones out of the hands of the CIA? Can you stop the signature strikes that are killing people on the basis of suspicious activities?"

Anyone following the Twitter feed of Hayes for coverage of the proceedings might have been under the impression that something truly magical had occurred, after Benjamin was dragged away by security. Let's say, for instance, you just got in from work and, knowing nothing about the situation, signed on to the social network. You would be confronted with an exuberant Hayes, telling his followers, "Seriously, the PRESIDENT OF THE UNITED STATES IS RIGHT NOW SAYING YOU SHOULD LISTEN TO MEDEA BENJAMIN."

Whoa! That's crazy! The President of the United States, the guy running a global assassination campaign that he will barely acknowledge exists, said that you should listen to a well-known antiwar activist! Right after she called him out in public no less. What a momentous occasion in our nation's history.

Imagine your disappointment when, after frantically searching for video of Benjamin's outburst, you learn that what the President actually said was this: "The voice of that woman is worth paying attention to.

Obviously I do not agree with much of what she said, and obviously she wasn't listening to me and much of what I said. But these are tough issues, and the suggestion that we can gloss over them is wrong."

This is, of course, vintage Obama. He first acknowledges the importance of Benjamin's position, before dismissing it, thus giving the impression that true discussion is taking place within our democracy. It's a trick that he's used countless times before, a ruse that apparently still fools Christopher Hayes, so much so that he hits Caps Lock. Medea Benjamin, clearly, wasn't protesting the specific words of Obama's speech; she was drawing attention to his policies, which tend to contradict nearly everything he has said about civilian drone deaths.

A quick perusal of Chris Hayes' Twitter feed leads to other moments of misplaced optimism and, guess what? They all involve the President. After Obama gave a speech on race following George Zimmerman's Not Guilty verdict, Hayes tweeted that it was "hard to imagine" Obama appointing, former NYPD Commissioner, Ray Kelly, whose department was infamous for its racist "Stop and Frisk" policy, as head at the Department of Homeland Security. WHY CHRIS HAYES? WHY WOULD THIS BE HARD TO IMAGINE? This is the same President who accepted a Nobel Peace Prize, then announced that thousands of additional troops would be sent to Afghanistan.

This kind of stuff begs a very basic question: does Chris Hayes really believe there is an operative connection between Obama's rhetorical acrobatics and the execution of his public policy and, if so, on what grounds does he base this belief? Certainly someone who has been paying close attention to politics, like Hayes (a journalist who covered Washington for a major liberal periodical before moving to television), knows that one of the most prominent criticisms leveled against Obama is the definitive separation between his talk and his walk. This disconnect began nearly as soon as he was elected President. Obama had made his position on the Iraq War a central component of his campaign against Hillary Clinton, arguing that Clinton was fundamentally incorrect about the biggest foreign policy disaster of our generation. Upon his election, Obama then selected her for the most important foreign policy gig in the world, excepting his own.

There were, of course, two ways to interpret this moment. The first is that Obama was skeptical of Clinton's hawkishness, but desired to set up some Team of Rivals cabinet, in which big ideas were debated and rational policy emerged. The second, and much more plausible, theory is that Barack Obama's opposition to the war in Iraq was never anything more than a political calculation and Clinton's exuberance for Bush's attack, perhaps, qualified her for such a position. After all, Obama's foreign policy ended up being a direct continuation of George W. Bush's.

This is an excellent segue to my favorite Chris Hayes moment of irrational analysis. In May of 2013, Barack Obama gave a speech at, historically black, Morehouse College, recycling the "pick yourself up the bootstraps" tropes of white conservatism and zeroing in on the perceived cultural ailments of a black audience. "We've got no time for excuses," said Obama, "not because the bitter legacies of slavery and segregation have vanished entirely; they haven't. Not because racism and discrimination no longer exist, that's still out there. It's just that in today's hyper-connected, hyper-competitive world, with a billion young people from China and India and Brazil entering the global workforce alongside you, nobody is going to give you anything you haven't earned. And whatever hardships you may experience because of your race, they pale in comparison to the hardships previous generations endured -- and overcame."

Succinct, and compelling, criticism of these lines was immediately doled out by the *Atlantic's* Ta-Nehisi Coates, "Taking the full measure of the Obama presidency thus far, it is hard to avoid the conclusion that this White House has one way of addressing the social ills that afflict black people -- and particularly black youth -- and another way of addressing everyone else. I would have a hard time imagining the president telling the women of Barnard that 'there's no longer room for any excuses' -- as though they were in the business of making them. Barack Obama is, indeed, the president of 'all America', but he also is singularly the scold of 'black America.'"[34]

Ah, but that's not what Chris Hayes saw at all: "President's commencement address to Morehouse is a really complicated, fascinating, personal speech." These are interesting words from the gentleman who believes social change will be led by the upper class.

The most telling Chris Hayes tweet was sent out during the debate on

Social Security, "Honest question for lefties who think Obama is horrible. Who do you see as better, more progressive American presidents?"

This question could be answered any number of ways, but it would be very easy to start with, say, Richard Nixon, perhaps our last liberal President if you quantify liberalism by domestic spending. Nixon accepted the Keynesian consensus of his era, investing vast sums of money into social programs, while passing landmark environmental legislation. In fact, anyone prior to Carter, the first candidate to tell America about the supposed miracle of "supply-side economics", was more progressive that Barack Obama. For the love of God, the tax-rate under Eisenhower was 90%. A fact that, presumably, invalidated any potential revolutions.

MELISSA HARRIS-PERRY:
Antiracist Neoliberal

"I am thrilled that President Obama has tapped Van Jones to serve as a special White House advisor. This appointment makes me think that Obama 'gets it' because Van Jones embodies a critically important political strategy for the left."

-Melissa Harris-Perry

"[Obama] will certainly govern to the center, because he campaigned to the center, but he also did it with a kind of transparency about where the money was going, and he did it, I think, ultimately, with a sense of wanting to include ordinary people's concerns and questions into these sort of big global processes."

-Melissa Harris-Perry

It would be a challenging task to determine which Obama-apology piece is the silliest and most offensive, but allow me to nominate Melissa Harris-Perry's, 2010 *Nation* column, "How Barack Obama is like Martin Luther King, Jr."

Perhaps the content of this particular effort is self-explanatory, but I will provide some context nonetheless: after a year of Obama disappointing African-Americans, many of whom believed that his victory would spark a long overdue discussion about the racism that permeates American culture, a handful of black intellectuals lobbed a few commonsensical criticisms at the President. One of these critiques came from, Georgetown professor, Dr. Michael Eric Dyson, who, during a television interview, explained, "I think that we should push the president. This president runs from race like a black man runs from a cop. What we have to do is ask Mr. Obama to stand up and use his bully pulpit to help us."

Melissa Harris-Perry, professor of political science at Tulane University and host of her own television show at MSNBC, took exception to Dyson's words and devoted her entire *Nation* column to the Herculean task of proving that Obama and MLK were, in fact, cut from the same cloth. "Often comparing Obama explicitly to Dr. King, [black intellectuals like Dyson] conclude the President lacks the moral courage or Leftist determination of the civil rights icon," assessed Harris-Perry. "I disagree. Barack Obama is stunningly similar to Martin Luther King, Jr., but to see this similarity we must relinquish the false, reconstructed memories of perfection we currently project onto King."

Dyson is an interesting target. This one comment notwithstanding, he was a vocal supporter of Barack Obama long before his election and has continued to defend him throughout the President's most questionable moments. During a 2012 debate with *Black Agenda Report's* Glen Ford, which aired on *Democracy Now*, Dyson argued that Obama was as good as it could possibly get, when it came to Presidents, "But the reality is, is that Obama is as progressive a figure who has the chance of being elected in America. Friedrich Engels is not going to be the secretary of labor, and Marx will not be the secretary of treasury, bottom line." In a May 2013 MSNBC interview, with Martin Bashir, Dyson referred to, Obama's Attorney General, Eric Holder as "the Moses of our time."

Harris-Perry then went on to define King as a pragmatic, and shrewd, civil rights leader: a man who turned his back on Bayard Rustin, because of his homosexuality, a guy who sold out the vision of Fannie Lou Hamer's Mississippi Freedom Party in order to maintain his political connections.

These are interesting tidbits to produce from the slain icon's biography (rather than say, citing the time he said America should move toward a democratic socialism) and they present a figure who can easily be transposed upon Obama's tepid brand of liberalism. "Barack Obama is not the leader of a progressive social movement; he is the president," wrote Melissa Harris-Perry, "As president he is both more powerful than Dr. King and more structurally constrained. He has more institutional power at his disposal and more crosscutting constituencies demanding his attention. He has more powerful allies and more powerful opponents."[35]

There's an inherent assumption that runs through these sentences, the idea that the objectives and goals of King and Obama are similar. This belief is, very often, a component of liberal apologetics for Obama; if the President is vouching for something detrimental, he is either being pressured by some dark, conservative force or he's simply attempting to navigate a grand bargain which will, ultimately, benefit everyone. "I see King in Obama," writes Harris-Perry, "a leader who is imperfectly, but wholeheartedly groping toward better and fairer solutions for our nation." So, when Obama stacks his economic team with some of the very people who brought about the most recent meltdown, or takes the single-payer option off the table as soon as he rolls out his healthcare plan, he is simply searching for equitable ways to assist the American people.

Harris-Perry's assessment of King is a tremendously disrespectful version of history. To hail a centrist President for following in King's footsteps flies in the face of nearly everything MLK stood for. Shortly before he was murdered, possibly by the state, King became a fierce critic of the Vietnam War, condemning the United States government as "the greatest purveyor of violence in the world." Contrast this with the actions of Barack Obama, who is running what Noam Chomsky has called, "the biggest terrorist operation that exists, maybe in history," the drone program which has killed scores of innocent civilians. Dr. Martin Luther King Jr. had a dream; President Obama has a Kill List.

On the 50th anniversary of MLK's March on Washington, a second rally was organized, featuring a speech from Obama, and enthusiastic coverage from MSNBC. The difference between the two marches highlighted the vast separation between the vision of King and that of Obama. In 1963,

President Kennedy had pleaded with King to call the whole thing off. Kennedy, a leader who dragged his feet on civil rights legislation, didn't think it was necessary to make such a big fuss about segregation and, like Harris-Perry, viewed outside agitators as possible hurdles to the political change they championed. Nick Bryant's definitive book on Kennedy's civil rights record is called *The Bystander* for a reason.

Cornel West, who has criticized Harris-Perry and others at MSNBC for selling their souls in exchange for Obama access, explained the irony of the 2013 march on *Democracy Now* "Brother Martin would not be invited to the very march in his name, because he would talk about drones. He'd talk about Wall Street criminality. He would talk about working class being pushed to the margins as profits went up for corporate executives in their compensation. He would talk about the legacies of white supremacy. Do you think anybody at that march will talk about drones and the drone president? Will you think anybody at that march will talk about the connection to Wall Street?"

Amy Goodman then asked if West had been invited to the march: "Well, can you imagine? Good God, no. I mean, I pray for him, because I'm for liberal reform. But liberal reform is too narrow, is too truncated. And, of course, the two-party system is dying, and therefore it doesn't have the capacity to speak to these kinds of issues."

Harris-Perry's unwavering belief that Obama is an agent for change, in the mold of King, also completely skips over the *actual* beginnings of Obama's political career, not the unbending subversive of the right's imagination, nor the noble community organizer that liberals embrace, but a shrewd operator who understood that the key to success in America is a firm, unwavering bond with moneyed interests. One of the only journalists to do the necessary digging on this end was, the late, Robert Fitch, who unearthed the inconvenient facts of Obama's early days in Chicago, explaining that, "If we examine more carefully the interests that Obama represents; if we look at his core financial supporters; as well as his inmost circle of advisors, we'll see that they represent the primary activists in the demolition movement and the primary real estate beneficiaries of this transformation of public housing projects into condos and townhouses: the profitable creep of the Central Business District and elite residential neighborhoods southward; and the shifting of the pile of human misery about three miles further into the South Side and the south suburbs."

Adolph Reed was another one of the few people who detected Obama's issues early. In his essay "The Curse of 'Community'", he wrote, "In Chicago, for instance, we've gotten a foretaste of the new breed of foundation-hatched black communitarian voices; one of them, a smooth Harvard lawyer with impeccable do-good credentials and vacuous-to-repressive neoliberal politics, has won a state senate seat on a base mainly in the liberal foundation and development worlds. His fundamentally bootstrap line was softened by a patina of the rhetoric of authentic community, talk about meeting in kitchens, small-scale solutions to social problems, and the predictable elevation of process over program-the point where identity politics converges with old-fashioned middle-class reform in favoring form over substance. I suspect that his ilk is the wave of the future in US black politics here, as in Haiti and wherever the International Monetary Fund has sway."[36]

When Harris-Perry was asked about her support of Barack Obama, during the 2008 campaign, within the context of the disappointments that came after, she proclaimed, "Oh, I am absolutely still a fierce endorser of President Obama and would make the same—would absolutely make the same choice within that truncated space that we have in the American political system. I guess what I'd say is, I'm a progressive in my—in my leanings and my preferences. I'm also, I suppose maybe from my years at the University of Chicago, a bit of a realist in my politics."

This unusual strain of realism has led Harris-Perry to embrace some truly wretched, and reactionary, policies. In 2012, in response to Chicago Mayor, and former Obama Chief of Staff, Rahm Emanuel's wave of teacher layoffs, the Chicago Teachers Union voted to authorize a strike, using the opportunity to highlight Emanuel's privatization agenda for Chicago's flailing schools. The CTU's demands, for better schools and fair pay, were presented over the backdrop of a tremendously segregated and poverty-stricken city; a cause that any self-respecting progressive should have jumped to support.

However, Harris-Perry perceived the Democratic attack on the Chicago Teachers Union as a struggle between, Chicago's elite political class "and teachers who are supposed to have their best interests at heart but who seem willing to allow this generation to be lost." Harris-Perry's conclusion established an equivalency between Emanuel's vicious educational policies and the striking workers, asserting a particularly dangerous interchangeability between the two sides.

"As one of the few pundits with a national platform willing to address the negative effects of income inequality, I was saddened by the framing Melissa Harris-Perry chose for her article," Kenzo Shibata, a Chicago activist, teacher, and co-founder of CORE: The Caucus of Rank-and-File Educators, told me. "What she failed to mention was that these were all measures being instituted by the powers that be, not by the teachers who walked the picket line for 7 days. She framed the piece as a war between two factions that left the public in the crossfire. However, if you saw the signs and heard the chants, you would have seen tens of thousands of educators and their supporters -- including parents and students --- calling for smaller class sizes, fully-resourced classrooms, and wraparound services for all students in need."

Harris-Perry's casual dismissal of the strike, coupled with her firm belief in ballot-box solutions, points to a worldview that disregards the importance of those fighting for a better America. Shibata explains, "No one wanted to the strike to happen. Teachers wanted to teach. Parents wanted their kids in school. Students wanted to learn. However, all shared sacrifice to stand up to a system that had been working against them for decades. The school days were made up, but the strike had a lasting impact in Chicago and the nation, changing the conversation and leading the way for a nationwide movement for strong public schools."

Harris-Perry has also written about the struggles Obama went through to pass the Affordable Health Care Act, sidestepping the inconvenient fact that it's a retread of the Heritage Foundation's plan from the mid-90s (which was created to squash a growing movement to establish a single-payer option) and criticizing those who advocated for universal healthcare as a lowly bloggers unable to understand the machinations of Washington policy.

Harris-Perry's act is a deceptive one: she defends worrisome legislation, and scoffs at legitimate activists, behind the guise of initiating a meaningful, and overdue, racial discussion. The fact she's an African-American, who regularly discusses race on MSNBC, lends a progressive sense of credibility to a President who has, at best, dragged his feet on issues of racial justice. John Halle summarizes the core of Harris-Perry's politics perfectly: "While giving pro forma nods to this or that aspect of the left agenda on the welfare state, the environment, and foreign intervention, her main focus and professional interest has always been race within a neoliberal framework defined by the Democratic Party implemented with consummate cynicism by the current administration. As such, matters such as, for example, the largest drop in African American wealth in history under an African-American president, grotesque rates of home foreclosures among African-American families are have elicited relatively little comment from her except as yet another policy failure to be laid at the feet of the Republicans."

The specific, and narrow, framework of Harris-Perry's outlook led her to work out a bizarre interpretation of left-wing Obama criticisms. Critiques of Obama from the left must be emerging from the same racist animus that fueled the right wing's slanders, she reasons. "The 2012 election may be a test of another form of electoral racism," wrote Harris-Perry, "the tendency of white liberals to hold African-American leaders to a higher standard than their white counterparts. If old-fashioned electoral racism is the absolute unwillingness to vote for a black candidate, then liberal electoral racism is the willingness to abandon a black candidate when he is just as competent as his white predecessors."[37]

Harris-Perry's assessment, and her implicit suggestion that the left was easier on President Clinton than they are on Obama, completely ignores the actual history. In reality, Clinton's reign was topped off by the massive WTO protest in Seattle, an inspiring populist rejection of the neoliberal economic order strangling the world. It was that shot of adrenaline that set the stage for over 2 million people pulling the lever for consumer advocate Ralph Nader, the Green Party candidate who identified the Bush/Gore battle as a depressing sham. On his blog, political scientist Corey Robin challenged Harris-Perry's lack of evidence regarding progressive racism towards Obama. "It occurred to me that there are five facts that Harris-Perry needs to establish that she nowhere establishes," wrote Robin. "I'd be satisfied if she could establish at least some of them, but she doesn't establish any of them. These are the facts that need to be established...

1. White liberals are significantly less supportive of Obama than they used to be.

2. The drop in white liberal support for Obama at this point is significantly greater than it was for Clinton at a comparable point (or frankly at any point) prior to his reelection.

3. The drop in white liberal support for Obama is significantly greater than the drop in black or Latino liberal support for Obama.

4. The differential among liberals between white and black or Latino support for Obama is significantly larger than the differential, if it existed, between white and black or Latino support for Clinton.

5. That larger differential, if it exists, is a reflection of declining white support for Obama rather than increasing or persistent black or Latino support for Obama.[38]

Harris-Perry's problem, as diagnosed by Robin in another post, transcends the contours of identity politics. "Unlike some folks, I don't think Harris-Perry's problem is her tendency to cry racism," wrote Robin, "No, it's far deeper than that. It's her tendency to reduce political arguments to psychological motivations...Psychology may or may not play a role in politics. But if it does, we need evidence-based psychologists, not fact-free astrologists, to explain it to us."

THE HOST IS THE MESSAGE
"We're the establishment."

Cenk Uygur, host of the popular progressive talk show, *The Young Turks*, seemed like the perfect fit for MSNBC. He was a burst of energy not seen since Olbermann manned his own program, a no-nonsense old-school lefty that would provide blistering critiques of our political culture. That was, presumably, the idea when MSNBC began using Uygur as a contributor on the network, and then gave him his own slot. The numbers looked good, as he earned first place in the 18-34 demographic during the second quarter of 2011. Nonetheless, Uygur was called into President Phil Griffin's office.

Uygur claims that Griffin told him "people in Washington" were concerned about his broadcasts. At the time, Uygur was easily the most left-wing host at the station, regularly criticizing Democrats, and the President. According to Uygur, Griffin spelled it out for him: "We're insiders. We're the establishment." After Uygur refused to be bumped to a less appealing time slot, MSNBC ended their contract with the host.

Uygur was floored. He assessed his reaction to Griffin's words during an interview, "My first reaction was, 'Wow, this is the speech.' This is the speech that people tell you about, but you thought you're never really gonna get, because usually it's a lot more subtle than that. You know, you'll get things like, 'oh, you really wanna do that story?' Or, 'you're sure about that?' But this was not subtle, this was the kind of thing you'd see in a movie. And my immediate reaction other than surprise was, 'well, I'm definitely not gonna do that.' So, we'll see if they really mean it or not, because I am gonna be just as tough on all the guests, and challenge them, and be just as tough on the Obama Administration as I always am, otherwise there's no point in doing the show. I don't need the money to do a show that I don't believe in. the whole reason I got into this business is so that we can deliver real information and truth to the audiences as best as we possibly can."

If this really happened, it's an amazing moment in MSNBC's history: it exposes the network's hand. Yes, every one who has watched MSNBC, since Olbermann's Katrina rant, has witnessed the rise of a specific culture and agenda but unlike a network like Fox, MSNBC leaves no trail. Again, this is what makes them so interesting. There's no coercion necessary at MSNBC, no leaked emails with marching orders from the Democratic Party. The people who work for the station are under the impression they possess a level of freedom unparalleled throughout our media landscape, but is Uygur's revelation surprising to anyone beyond the confines of the station's Manhattan address?

This is a network that debated whether or not President Obama's face should be added to Mount Rushmore. During that rousing and important discussion, Touré, ever the skeptic, told Al Sharpton that, he wouldn't agree to chiseling in Barack's face until he finished his "fundamental transformation" of America, including gun control and gay rights. But wait, they've had this debate more than once! Chris "Thrill Going Up My Leg" Matthews opined that Obama maybe shouldn't be added to Rushmore but probably, "The level right below it." Another memorable MSNBC argument took place when *The Cycle* addressed an apparent controversy, which had arisen after host Steve Kornacki failed to refer to "President Obama" a few times, instead referencing "Obama." Confused? MSNBC was not. They spent over 5 minutes breaking down whether or not omitting the word "President" from his title was disrespectful.

MSNBC is, quite obviously, a wing of the establishment. At least Phil Griffin seems to realize it, unlike his employees. The station demonstrates its obvious bias when they hire Former White House press secretary Robert Gibbs as a contributor, or they sign up White House senior advisor and senior strategist for President Obama's 2008 and 2012 campaigns, David Axelrod to provide viewers with political analysis. Recently, MSNBC announced that they have hired Ronan Farrow, a former Obama foreign policy official, to host a weekday show. According to a Pew study, conducted during the tail end of the 2012 election, 71% of the stories MSNBC did on Republican candidate Mitt Romney were negative and, yes, it would be nearly impossible to run a positive story on someone like Romney, but compare it to Fox, a mere 46% of the stories they did on Obama, during the same period, were negative.

The essence of Griffin's declaration is not always completely apparent. For every deliberation on what level of Mount Rushmore His Excellency's face should end up on, there's some connection to the ruling class obscured to the naked eye. Take the case of Ari Melber. He's currently a co-host on MSNBC's *The Cycle* and a correspondent for *The Nation*. He worked for Secretary of State John Kerry and, Washington Senator (and Iraq war supporter) Maria Cantwell before coming to MSNBC. He's also an associate at the law firm Cahill, Gordon, and Rendell. On his website, Melber writes, "I think that disclosures can advance transparency and enable readers to factor in additional information when assessing a writer's work. I am a practicing attorney, and do not publicly comment on or write about my clients."

This is, indeed, true. Search Melber's website as extensively as you desire, you won't find any information regarding Cahill, Gordon, & Rendell, much less the work they do, or the clients they represent. For instance, you will see no mention of his assistance to partner Floyd Abrams, a free speech advocate who once declared, "I don't spend my life simply working for the ACLU." You'll find no information regarding them representing the National Cable & Telecommunications Association or Time Warner. You won't see anything on his website explaining how, him and Abrams, prepared a letter to the House Judiciary Committee defending the Stop Online Piracy Act (SOPA). Nowhere on the website will you notice any indication that they prepared a letter to the Senate Judiciary Committee arguing the merits of the Combating Online Infringement and Counterfeits Act (COICA).

You'll recall that the movement against SOPA, a piece of legislation that would have severely scaled back the democratic nature of the internet, generated the largest online protest in history, with over 115,000 websites going black to highlight the importance of killing the legislation. Prior to the backlash, *The Nation's* "net movement correspondent" didn't write about one of the biggest net movements ever. By the way, *The Nation's* Net movement correspondent is Ari Melber. Another aspect to this wonderful spectacle was summarized nicely in a blog post, "Abrams/Melber client Time Warner was among the largest donors to Obama's 2012 campaign. So was Comcast, which in addition to being a member company of the group for which Abrams and Melber petitioned the FCC, also co-owns MSNBC and CNBC, where Melber is a paid contributor." But don't worry everyone, Melber does "not make financial donations to political candidates", preferring objectivity of course.[39]

The aforementioned traits are not initially detectable in the being of Richard Wolffe either, an MSNBC contributor and frequent guest host at the station. Wolffe is part of Public Strategies Inc., a corporate communications firm, run by Dan Bartlett, George W. Bush's White House Communications Director. As Glenn Greenwald wrote at the time, "Having Richard Wolffe host an MSNBC program — or serving as an almost daily 'political analyst' – is exactly tantamount to MSNBC's just turning over an hour every night to a corporate lobbyist. Wolffe's role in life is to advance the P.R. interests of the corporations that pay him, including corporations with substantial interests in virtually every political issue that MSNBC and Countdown cover. Yet MSNBC is putting him on as a guest-host and "political analyst" on one of its prime-time political shows. What makes that even more appalling is that, as Ana Marie Cox, neither MSNBC nor Wolffe even disclose any of this."[40]

Now let's compare and contrast the shilling here. Phil Griffin, President of a mainstream network, is fully aware of the fact MSNBC has developed itself into a brand, an alluring piece of scenery for the elite. This is what he aspired to build all along. "Every time I met somebody from Fox, I tried to get a debrief of how he runs that operation," Griffin told the *New Republic*. Such an operation requires deep pockets and strong connections to power. This is something his employees and ex-employees, with the exception of Uygur, seem completely unaware of, but if you dig deep enough on any issue, the problematic nature of MSNBC begins to formulate. For instance, MSNBC has actually run some really good pieces on climate change and has covered the environment better than most networks, which is to say, they have covered it at all. However, when they revamped their website, (calling it "Platform for the Lean Forward, progressive community") they funded it via native ads for America's Natural Gas Alliance and General Electric. As reporter Steve Horn writes, those providing these ads are, "fully invested in the fossil fuel industry, with assets in fracking, coal, offshore drilling, tar sands, and more. ANGA is the shale gas industry's lobbying tour de force, both at the federal and state level." Follow the money, as the cliché goes.[41]

And speaking of money, before suspending him, for the crime of exhibiting bias by donating money to political campaigns, MSNBC aimed to squash the infamous beef between Keith Olbermann and Bill O'Reilly. According to a story by Brian Stelter, which ran in the *New York Times,* Jeffrey Immelt, the chairman of General Electric had something of a summit with Rupert Murdoch, media mogul and owner of Fox News. It was orchestrated by, of all people, Charlie Rose. Stelter's story details how, "The reconciliation — not acknowledged by the parties until now — showcased how a personal and commercial battle between two men could create real consequences for their parent corporations. A G.E. shareholders' meeting, for instance, was overrun by critics of MSNBC (and one of Mr. O'Reilly's producers) last April . . . .In late 2007, Mr. O'Reilly had a young producer, Jesse Watters, ambush Mr. Immelt and ask about GE's business in Iran, which is legal, and which includes sales of energy and medical technology. G.E. says it no longer does business in Iran...Over time, G.E. and the News Corporation concluded that the fighting "wasn't good for either parent," said an NBC employee with direct knowledge of the situation. But the session hosted by Mr. Rose provided an opportunity for a reconciliation, sealed with a handshake between Mr. Immelt and Mr. Murdoch."[42]

There it is, ladies and gentlemen: the true scandal of our modern media in all its abysmal glory. The issue has never been whether the media is too liberal or too conservative, the problem is *who controls the media.* Someone, somewhere, finds the content of MSNBC useful, and the only thing that impedes its usefulness is a turn of events that challenges its shareholders' bottom line. Right/left narrative continues to dominate MSNBC's programming. After Barack Obama's reelection in 2012, Rachel Maddow went on triumphant rant, declaring a possible victory for the forces of reason. The network's preferred candidate had seemingly sailed to victory with ease, lapping an uninspiring Republican nominee who reminded most Americans of how much they hated their boss.

"Listen, last night was a good night for liberals and for Democrats for very obvious reasons, but it was also, possibly, a good night for this country as a whole. Because in this country, we have a two- party system in government," Maddow explained. "And the idea is supposed to be that the two sides, both come up with ways to confront and fix the real problems facing our country. They both propose possible solutions to our real problems and we debate between those possible solutions. And by the process of debate, we pick the best idea. That competition between good ideas from both sides about real problems in the real country should result in our country having better choices, better options, than if only one side is really working on the hard stuff."

Maddow's contention that Democrats have been "working on the hard stuff," imagines a fully functioning democracy. Perhaps she believes Barack Obama was working on the hard stuff when he generated a healthcare plan nearly identical to Bob Dole's from 1996, then immediately gutted all the reproductive health stuff when the right, predictably, made a stink. Perhaps she believes

Maddow continued, "Last night the Republicans got shellacked, and they had no idea it was coming. And we saw them in real-time, in real humiliating time, not believe it, even as it was happening to them. And unless they are going to is secede, they are going to have to pop the factual bubble they have been so happy living inside if they do not want to get shellacked again, and that will be a painful process for them, but it will be good for the whole country, left, right, and center."

In Maddow's world, the election boiled down to a very clear choice: embrace the unparalleled stupidity of the GOP or side with the levelheaded Democrats. Maddow's show is, primarily, viewed by people who share her politics, so she isn't actually addressing GOP members here; she's patting her base on the back for their exuberant support of prudent leaders. This is a variation of support that contained virtually no caveats, during the election season, and made no noticeable demands on a man who extended Bush tax cuts and doubled down on his foreign policy decisions.

Yes, sure, the country has made great strides socially and this was reflected in many results throughout the nation on that November evening, but what about the overall state of the union? If people who think dinosaurs walked the earth with humans and Obama's healthcare plan signaled a return of the Red Menace are the ones clogging up the gears of democracy, distracting the population from the very real problems at hand then, pray tell, what are those dilemmas? What "constructive debate about competing feasible ideas" is being concealed from the American people and, if these evil miscreants are so far removed from reality, then why does MSNBC spend so much time covering them?

After, antiwar activist, Medea Benjamin interrupted an Obama speech on drones, calling for Maddow ran a graphic reading, "Stop Agreeing with Me!" the implication being that, if Benjamin just shut up and listened, she would quickly learn that Obama had many of the same reservations. What kind of nonsense is this? Clearly, Barack Obama has virtually no connection to the domestic left, so why the insistence on pretending he's some sort of great liberal? Furthermore, why is the Tea Party consistently presented, by MSNBC, as some sort of plodding gang of nutjobs, free of any necessary context? The Tea Party, much like the Occupy Movement, started with a sizable cultural reverberation and, then, began something of a skid. Discussion about whether or not there is any definitive difference between mainstream Republicans and Tea Party-backed candidates. During the government shutdown, the media as Anthony DiMaggio, author of *The Rise of the Tea Party,* told me, "The voting record differences between Tea Party and non-Tea Party Republicans in Congress don't appear to be significantly different, according to the research that's been done. That means that the polarization of the Republican Party further to the right is bigger than simply a Tea Party phenomenon."

This is an important point consistently overlooked by MSNBC's coverage of the current GOP. There is an, assumption, embedded into nearly all Maddow's commentary on the Tea Party, that they represent a new variant of right-wing wackiness previously unknown to American politics. History, certainly, does not reflect that. As the historian Rick Perlstein has written, "Over fifteen years of studying the American right professionally — especially in their communications with each other, in their own memos and media since the 1950s — I have yet to find a truly novel development, a real innovation, in far-right 'thought.'"[43]

While Maddow and the gang consistently fillet the Sarah Palins of the world, the ship remains steady and the checks continue to be signed. In case you are wondering, Al Sharpton, a former Democratic Presidential candidate, and a man who has publicly vowed to never criticize the President, replaced Uygur.

THE BETRAYAL OF CHELSEA MANNING AND EDWARD SNOWDEN

"Man is not what he thinks he is, he is what he hides."

-André Malraux

By now, you know the story of Chelsea Manning, the former Private who leaked a treasure trove of documents to the America public, with the assistance of Wikileaks. You know that, she entered America's "War on Terror" with grandiose notions, yet quickly became disillusioned with her country's objectives and tactics. You know that she was given clearance to view scores of classified material and was shocked by what she saw. You know that she was privy to the details of crimes that she believed the American people should know about. You know that she went to the *New York Times* and *Washington Post*, believing that our major newspapers would have some level of interest in the material. You know that, somewhere along the way, she began confiding in Adrian Lamo, a well-known hacker who was working with the FBI. You know that Lamo ratted her out. You know she was subjected to solitary confinement, then a proceeding that had all the makings of a show trial, before being sentenced to 35 years behind bars.

Media coverage of Manning has been consistently vexatious for a multitude of reasons, most recently because the whistleblower, formerly known as Bradley Manning, announced that she identified as a woman. This statement ignited a storm of transphobic bilge, including a depressing argument about whether, or not, the press should continue referring to her with male pronouns. Before that, the press dropped the ball by regularly presenting the story as the tale of some misguided soul. Manning dumped documents, the narrative went, without fully understanding what was in them, thus potentially putting a number of people's lives in danger. This argument gained some level of traction because it depended upon the inability, of Manning supporters, to prove a negative: since we are dealing with such classified material, and subjects, no one could *really* prove that the leak hadn't led to some level of death and destruction, in some corner of the world. As for the idea that the American people have a right to know what their government does throughout the world, it was almost never even broached. As Chase Madar, author of *The Passion of Bradley Manning: The Story of the Suspect Behind the Largest Security Breach in U.S. History*, told me when I interviewed him, "What I find truly depressing...is that all of this vital information was easily available for years but nobody, until... Manning, saw fit to leak it. Mind you I don't see leaks as a problem I see them as a partial solution. We need to know what our government is doing, especially in time of war."[44]

However, the most aggravating aspect of the Manning coverage wasn't what was written, it was what was omitted. Stories on Manning's fate, and debates on how she should have been punished, almost always eschewed any deeper analysis of her leaks or the national debate she believed they would kick off. Manning's name became synonymous with the "Collateral Murder" video, a tape of cockpit footage which showed American soldiers killing over a dozen civilians, including three men who were attempting to assist the victims. This was an extremely disturbing clip, which lifted the veil off the supposed "liberation of Iraq" and exposed the operation for the brutal attack that it was. Daniel Ellsberg, who Manning is frequently compared to, summarized the horror of the video, "It would be interesting to have someone speculate or tell us exactly what context would lead to justifying the killing that we see on the screen. As the killing goes on, you obviously would see the killing of men who are lying on the ground in an operation where ground troops are approaching and perfectly capable of taking those people captive, but meanwhile you're murdering before the troops arrive. That's a violation of the laws of war and of course what the mainstream media have omitted from their stories is this context."

This is all true, but the video is just the tip of the iceberg in terms of what Manning actually leaked. She revealed that Israel wanted to bring Gaza to "the brink of collapse", that the Afghan vice president left the country with $52 million, that Shell has "inserted staff" in Nigeria's government, that the US knew about Tunisia corruption and went on supporting the regime, that the US knew the 2009 Honduras coup was unconstitutional, that Egyptian torturers were trained by the FBI, that the President of Yemen ran cover for the US and pretended their attacks on the country were the work of his government, and a multitude of additional facts which should have generated a healthy level of skepticism towards the country's ruling class. Yes here, in all its glory, was the Empire, it's dirty secrets, and embarrassing connections exposed by one if its own. Manning's leaks were a much-needed dose of reality, in contrast to the popular belief in benign American intention or the depressing post-9/11 conspiracy mongering that grips entire sectors of the left.

The United States government was dealt another impressive blow during the spring of 2013, after *The Guardian* published a series of stories based on the leaks of Edward Snowden, a former Booz Hamilton employee with disturbing details regarding the scope of the National Security Agency's spying program. Snowden had thought about leaking material prior to 2013, but held off because he "believed in Obama's promises." After Obama continued many of his predecessor's policies, Snowden felt compelled to share his information with the world. "The 4th and 5th Amendments to the Constitution of my country, Article 12 of the Universal Declaration of Human Rights, and numerous statutes and treaties forbid such systems of massive, pervasive surveillance," reasoned Snowden, but the government had no time for a civics lesson, and charged Snowden with espionage and theft.

Prominent voices on the right, predictably, opined that the two individuals should be severely punished. Bill O'Reilly and Geraldo Rivera agreed that Manning should get over 20 years, neoconservative shill-journo Jamie Kirchick argued that Manning should be put to death, a view that was shared by at least one presidential candidate. "Whoever in our government leaked that information is guilty of treason, and I think anything less than execution is too kind a penalty," Mike Huckabee told reporters during a stop at the Ronald Reagan Library to promote, his kid's book, "Can't Wait Till Christmas!"

However, many on the left remained silent, unable to process the situation. Manning and Snowden were taking aim, not just at a specific political party or persuasion, but at the entire structure of our government. In many ways, it was reminiscent of the right/left reaction to a military attack after 9/11. While the right advocated demolishing Afghanistan in the name of revenge, and erecting a monument depicting Bush riding a bald eagle, progressives struggled to justify an indiscriminate bombing campaign. Sure, all their criticisms of American power remained valid but, when push came to shove, they lacked the courage of their convictions. By the same token, the right had no problem calling for the imprisonment and death of whistleblowers, in order to protect the surveillance-state they regularly defended, but the left was faced with a much deeper existential dilemma: the Manning/Snowden leaks focused a spotlight on many things they regularly complained about, but their actions went a step further.

Liberals quickly developed a tactic to combat this problem: change the subject. What was up with Manning's sexuality? Hadn't she had numerous discipline problems while in the military? What countries were willing to welcome the exiled Edward Snowden? What were the human rights records of the countries that were willing to take the whistleblower in? Yes, these individuals forced progressives into a conundrum, but if they simply focused on the personal lives of Manning and Snowden, they could easily divert attention from wider issues of transparency, lies, theft, and murder. This strategy certainly had precedent. It's worth remembering that Richard Nixon aimed to dismiss the importance of the *Pentagon Papers* leak by attacking Ellsberg personally. "Don't worry about his trial," he told Henry Kissinger and John Mitchell. "Just get everything out and try him in the press...I want to destroy him in the press. Is that clear?"

Nixon's quest to sully the reputation of Ellsberg, led to the formation of his own personal pack of Brownshirts; a group dubbed The Plumbers. The illegal shenanigans perpetrated by the covert White House Unit led, of course, to the Watergate scandal. Gordon Liddy, chief operative for The Plumbers, suggested his fellow gang members read Ellsberg's PhD thesis, "Risk, Ambiguity, and Decision," figuring that it would provide a glimpse into Ellsberg's ethical outlook. The group also sought out information on those who consorted with Ellsberg. "If there is no conspiracy," asked Special Assistant at the National Security Council David Young, "what are the motives which bring together the individuals involved? Is it that they want to get control or exercise power? Do they have nefarious motives?"

Assigning nefarious motives to Manning wasn't especially difficult. She had yet to reveal that she identified as a woman and, when the story first broke, analysis of her leaks were tinged with a certain level of homophobia. MSNBC contributor, and frequent guest-host, Joy Reid argued that the lecherous leaker wasn't some hero but just, "a guy seeking anarchy as a salve for his own personal, psychological torment." Those war crimes he exposed? Just a gay kid lashing out. Reid's farcical analysis was, actually, some of the only commentary on the subject, from an MSNBC personality. The network barely covered the proceedings.

In the case of Snowden, there was a more sizable amount of coverage, but a consistent inference emanated from MSNBC that wasn't entirely specific. MSNBC was not entirely sure if there was an operative connection between Snowden and Russian President Vladimir Putin, nor were they arguing that Glenn Greenwald, the journalist who Snowden leaked to, was connected to these hypothetical conspiracies, they were just asking questions. One is reminded of Nixon again: "I do not, like some people, believe my opponent is a Communist..."

When WikiLeaks spokesperson Kristinn Hrafnsson appeared on MSNBC's *Now with Alex Wagner*, he faced a swarm of accusatory questions from Joy Reid, in a segment that had the feel of a trial.

Reid: Obviously the most important question...is Edward Snowden still holed up in the Moscow airport?

Hrafnsson: I can't reveal his exact location or his travel plans.

Reid: The Russians have revealed his exact location. They said he was in the Moscow airport. Wikileaks is paying for his travel. Do you guys not know where he is?

Hrafnsson: We of course know where he is. We do have a hand in paying for his travel from Hong Kong to Moscow, that is correct.

Reid: If he were to travel on to the next country, he's half indicated he wants to go to South America, Wikileaks would pay for that too?

Hrafnsson: That remains to be seen.

Reid: But if you didn't pay for it, who would? Isn't Wikileaks providing him with legal counsel? Someone traveling with him?"

Hrafnsson: There is a legal aide on his behalf traveling with him. He has access to persons on our legal team and we did connect our legal team with his legal advisors.

Reid: Who's paying for those legal advisors?

Hrafnsson: Our legal advisers? Some we are paying ourselves and some are working pro bono.

Reid: I wonder if there was money from -- there is an organization that raises money for Wikileaks – Freedom of the Press Foundation – is that organization involved in paying for Mr. Snowden's travel?

Hrafnsson: The money that we have access to comes from various sources. One is the Freedom of the Press Foundation. We have a fund in France as well that's collecting money on our behalf. despite the banking block on us. We have funds in Iceland from (the period) prior to the banking blockade against the organization.

Reid: I ask that question because two journalists obviously Mr. Snowden gave some of the leaked information to are on the board of the Freedom of the Press Foundation. Were you aware of that when Wikileaks began paying for his travel?

Reid: I want to get you to react to something Lonnie Snowden, Mr. Snowden's father, said. He essentially said 'I don't want him to put him in peril,' meaning his son, 'but i am concerned about those who surround him. I think Wikileaks if you look at its past history you know that the focus is not necessarily on the constitution of the United States, it's simply to release as much information as possible.' What's your reaction to that?

Hrafnsson: I think Mr. Snowden senior has been rather ill-informed by mainstream media in this country and he has no accurate information about the organization. We are concerned about human rights. We are concerned about the freedom of speech and --

Reid: But he mentioned the U.S. Constitution.

Hrafnsson: Where the U.S. Constitution pertains to these issues we would support the U.S. Constitution.

Reid: Let me ask you whether or not Edward Snowden was ill-informed about Wikileaks in 2009. When he was in a chat room overseas he essentially accused the New York Times – we're gonna put up the graphic – that was his screen name. 'thetruehooha' he was calling himself, he was talking about a previous leak in a January 10, 2009 report that President Bush turned down a request from Israelis for bunker busting bombs that it wanted to use to attack iran's main nuclear site. he put up 'wtf, new york times, are they trying to start a war? Jesus Christ, they're like Wikileaks.' Then he talked about anonymous sources, he said those people should be shot in the chicarrones. Was he essentially ill-informed as well when he said essentially 'the New York Times' was like Wikileaks in a bad way for leaking information?

.

Hrafnsson: It has not been confirmed this is actually from Mr. Snowden.

Reid: Actually, it has been confirmed.

Hrafnsson: If so, he's obviously changed his position in 2009 and every person should be allowed to change his opinion in a positive way as he has done.

Reid: I want to open it up to the panel. One of the additional countries added to the potential country hopping that Mr. Snowden is doing is Venezuela, which has said they'd gladly accept Mr. Snowden. So now we have a trifecta of countries that might not be the most savory, in addition to Ecuador.

The spirit of Joe McCarthy lives deep in the heart of Joy Reid, who polishes off her insinuations regarding Snowden's shadowy funders with a swipe at Venezuela, a country guilty of possessing the temerity to stand up to the Washington consensus. Didn't she read that part of the Chris Hayes book about all the people voting against the IMF? At this point, Reid brought Melissa Harris-Perry into the discussion, wrapping up a truly embarrassing moment in the network's short history. As Bruce Dixon, of *Black Agenda Report,* explained it "At this point, the heads of both prosecutor Reid and tough cop Harris-Perry simultaneously imploded. They both lost it, unintelligibly shouting over each other for more than ten seconds. After they stopped shouting, Hrafsson tried to say the issue was the substance of Snowden's revelations, that the US government was illegally collecting, literally every email, text message, phone call, facebook post and electronic brain fart on the planet and storing it for future data-mining reference. Bad cop Harris-Perry would have none of it, angrily declaring that the issues were Snowden's illegitimacy, because he won't turn himself in, and his possible contact with foreign countries who might mean "to do us harm...Prosecutor Reid replied to the Nixon quote with unintentional irony, asserting that Snowden didn't reveal any illegal behavior, because of course the government had done nothing illegal, and as host, ended the segment...The camera cut away quickly, maybe so we couldn't see the Wikileaks guy laughing."[45]

Harris-Perry upped the ante for cringe-worthy Snowden segments, a short time later, when she read an open letter to the whistleblower at the end of her show. She addressed Snowden shortly before he ended up in Russia and used the opportunity to suggest a location for the young man. "It's me, Melissa," she began. "I hear you're looking for a country. Well, wouldn't you know, I have an idea for you! How about...this one?"

Harris-Perry's letter to Snowden addressed the mainstream media's failure to adequately explain the NSA revelations to the American public, but placed the blame at the feet of the leaker. "By engaging in this Tom Hanks-worthy, border-jumping drama," she explained, "through some of the world's most totalitarian states, you're making yourself the story.... We could be talking about whether accessing and monitoring citizen information and communications is constitutional, or whether we should continue to allow a secret court to authorize secret warrants using secret legal opinions.

But we're not. We're talking about you! And flight paths between Moscow and Venezuela, and how much of a jerk Glenn Greenwald is. We could at least be talking about whether the Obama administration is right that your leak jeopardized national security. But we're not talking about that, Ed....We're talking about you. I can imagine you'd say, well then stop! Just talk about something else. But here's the problem, even if your initial leak didn't compromise national security, your new cloak and dagger game is having real and tangible geopolitical consequences. So, well, we have to talk about...you."

So Melissa Harris-Perry, a progressive journalist, claims that her silence on the important NSA leaks provided by Edward Snowden can be blamed on...Edward Snowden. Snowden's refusal to return home and face the music (a recent liberal euphemism for the phrase "lengthy jail sentence") incapacitates media members from talking about a, possibly illegal, spying program run by the Obama administration. But here's a funny thing: it turns out that, every now and again, "facing the music" might actually constitute torture. That's according to, UN special rapporteur on torture, Juan Mendez who launched a 14-month investigation into the treatment of Chelsea Manning and, quite obviously, concluded that being in solitary confinement 23 hours a day over an 11-month period is pretty fucking cruel and inhumane. It's not entirely surprising if Harris-Perry is completely unaware of Manning's treatment, because her network barely covered the proceedings, but to claim that Snowden would receive a fair trial because so many people are aware of his case, is an assertion completely invalidated by what happened to Manning.

Manning, like Snowden, had a vast number of supporters who protested her treatment on a regular basis. In fact, a group of them confronted President Obama after a fundraiser, prior to Manning's trial, and asked him about the young Private's future. Obama told them, "I have to abide by certain classified information. If I was to release stuff, information that I'm not authorized to release, I'm breaking the law. … We're a nation of laws. We don't individually make our own decisions about how the laws operate. … He broke the law."

The President of the United States already had his mind made up, on whether Manning was innocent or guilty, before the trial began, as did the various offshoots of government authority, which cracked down on Manning supporters. Homeland Security officials detained David House, a supporter of Manning, on his way back from Mexico. After being held without charges or explanation, the agents snatched House's laptop, which he was only able to get back after he sued the US government. I talked to him shortly after the incident and he spoke of a climate of fear that had permeated the lives of Manning supporters. When I asked him about visiting Manning, after she was transferred from Kuwait to Virginia, he told me, "You should've seen the shithole they were keeping [her] in, what it was doing to [her]. That and the isolation."

This all happened with a hardly a word broadcast from MSNBC, the biggest military trial of this generation was barely even covered by, supposed outlier, Chris Hayes. Surely, by Harris-Perry's logic, an outfit like MSNBC should have been able to vigorously analyze the monumental nature of Manning's leaks and provide illuminating coverage of such a historic event. Manning was notIn fact, when Manning pled guilty to some of the charges leveled against her, on February 28 2013, MSNBC didn't even cover the plea at all. As Kevin Gosztola, of *FireDogLake* wrote at the time, "Rachel Maddow used her program on February 28 to cover the sequester, GOP opposition to the Violence Against Women Act, Democrats versus the NRA, Pope Benedict and also promoted her appearance on *The Daily Show* with Jon Stewart. Lawrence O'Donnell used his program on February 28 to cover the sequester, GOP opposition to the Violence Against Women Act, Speaker John Boehner, three Democrats who plan to 'tax Wall Street' and the Obama administration weighing in on Proposition 8. Ed Schultz used his program to cover Bob Woodward's claims about the Obama administration, the Supreme Court and voting rights, the Subway co-founder's opposition to Obamacare, Eric Cantor's threat of GOP "civil war," religious fundamentalist Pat Robertson talking about 'demons' in 'sweaters' and Pope Benedict."[46]

A bit of explanation on that last tidbit. Pat Robertson, a man who blamed the 9/11 attacks on gays and abortionists, was answering a question about a viewer's mother. The mom was concerned that items, purchased at the Salvation Army, may contain the remnants of sin. What if, say, a nonbeliever had allowed the sprit of Satan to permeate his, or her, sweatshirt before handing it over to Goodwill? Was some sort of exorcism necessary to rid the garments of their possible possession?

Obviously, Schultz's audience is not made up of the kind of people who would watch Pat Robertson's program and, so, the question arises: what possible function does such a segment have at a network like MSNBC? It's quite clear that, it's only possible use is that of a knowing wink to MSNBC's base, to remind them that they're intellectually superior to the kind of people concerned about whether or not there are demons in their clothes, not unlike the chorus of cheers that descends upon Bill Maher's panel when a liberal guest says anything. MSNBC has producers and writers who sit down at the beginning of the day, peruse the top stories, and decide what will be covered and what will be omitted. At a certain point, during such a proceeding, it is plausible that while looking over the days headlines, someone in Ed Schultz's crew declared, "Hey, Manning just pled guilty. This is a massively important trial, especially when put within the context of the Obama administration's War on Whistleblowers. The Democrats are, in fact, the political party in charge right now and, perhaps, a consistent focus on the opposition party's more farcical members does a vast disservice to our viewers, in that it presents a tremendously skewed view of the news." If so, this person was shot down and told, "We have no time. We need to cover these demon sweaters."

Obama's War on Whistleblowers cuts to the core of MSNBC's limitations. Yes, like conservatives, liberals now have a network that espouses their viewpoints, but liberalism's truncated prescription for change is predicated on tinkering. Liberals look out their windows and see a society that can be fundamentally shifted through incremental changes: reallocation of military spending, investment in infrastructure, market-based solutions to climate change, and more tax-breaks for the middle-class. Whistleblowers like Manning and Snowden point to a much deeper rot by suggesting, through their leaks, that the entire system is in desperate need of an overhaul.

****

As this book goes to print, the Obama administration is contemplating an attack on Syria, a country where over 100,000 people have been killed in civil war, The prospect of yet another doomed US entanglement in the Middle East produced single digit support numbers from the American public and skepticism began to form on both sides of the aisle. McCain's disregard for protocol was easy to mock, but it symbolized the futility of the "debate": McCain had made up his mind on intervention long before taking out his Blackberry and the proceedings were, quite obviously, a mere political calculation meant to boost up the sagging approval for another war.

Yes, of course, many in the GOP were simply against any intervention in Syria because it was Obama's idea, but many of them were, also, responding to the pressure of their constituents. As the Obama administration greased the gear of war, rolling out Secretary of State John Kerry to make a number of cringe-worthy World War 2 comparisons, Rachel Maddow explained to her audience exactly how horrible the world would be if...John McCain had been elected President.

Yes, while an international debate was raging over what to do about Syrian dictator Bashar Assad's use of chemical weapons, Maddow ran an entire segment wondering how many wars a President McCain would have waged. She put a map up on the screen, pointing out every country that

McCain had criticized until, it was implied, most of the world would have been invaded.

What possible function could such a segment have, beyond explaining to the viewer that, despite his murderous foreign policy, a Democrat President is still preferable to a Republican one? Couldn't the exercise easily be reversed? A world in which the United States has bases throughout the world, occupies countries, and engages in clandestine activities against elected governments need not be a hypothetical and humorous segment: it's happening right now. Would a President McCain, like President Obama, possess a "Kill List", full of individuals designated for assassination? Would a President McCain have killed American citizen Anwar al-Awlaki, without a trial, then murdered his 16-year-old son, who had left home in search of his father, a short time later?

It's also interesting that Maddow, someone who wrote an entire book on national security, is under the impression that every foreign policy statement made by McCain would have manifested itself in subsequent policy, had he been elected. After all, everyone knows that FDR ran for President on a platform that included a promise to stay out of Europe. The same can be said about LBJ, who branded himself as a peace candidate, while framing Goldwater as a warmonger ready to blow up the world. In both scenarios, the foreign policy of these men was defined in direct contradiction to what they ran on, so why is Maddow so sure that McCain would possess the means, and political clout, to do all the things he referenced?

There's something else that must be considered if we are going to have a discussion about the horrors of an imaginary McCain presidency: the sudden death of the American antiwar movement. As David Sirota wrote, in a piece titled "What Happened to the Antiwar Movement?", the driving force behind the death robust war criticism was, in fact, the election of Barack Obama in 2008. "This is red-versus-blue tribalism in its most murderous form," wrote Sirota. "It suggests that the party affiliation of a particular president should determine whether or not we want that president to kill other human beings. It further suggests that we should all look at war not as a life-and-death issue, but instead as a sporting event in which we blindly root for a preferred political team."[47]

The numbers back up Sirota's assertion. According to a study conducted by University of Michigan's Michael Heaney and colleague Fabio Rojas of Indiana University, the antiwar movement was demobilized by Obama's victory in 2008. Bush's decision to attack Iraq had, seemingly, reinvigorated the American antiwar movement and, in many ways, opened up the space necessary for Obama's presidential run. As, none other than, Chris Hayes wrote, "Obama only had a fighting chance at the nomination because of the credibility bestowed by his appearance at a 2002 rally opposing the invasion of Iraq, where he referred to the impending invasion as a 'dumb war'. When all the smart people got it wrong, including his many rivals for the nomination, he got it right. He, alone among the leading contenders, was able to see that the emperor had no clothes. Hillary Clinton and her husband came to symbolize the Establishment, and Barack Obama was there to dislodge it. He invoked, time and time again, the great social movements in American history that attacked the authority of the unjust institutions that preserved the status quo. And he advanced a critique of American politics at the end of the Bush years that homed in on the fundamental dysfunctions, improper dependencies, and imbalances of power that had led to the mess we were in."

Obama's warmongering was ignored by most anti-Bush liberals who, seemingly, viewed the impact of America's foreign policy through the spectrum of tribalism. The antiwar rallies that used to produce hundreds of young people, now bring together dozens. The bombs that progressives used to believe damaged our international standing are now met with shrugs. This attitude goes far beyond the President's foreign policy and envelopes nearly all his actions. There has been a certain level of disappointment expressed by Obama supporters who feel as if he failed to keep his promises on key issues, but very little analysis about the horrible things he actually delivered on. Obama's foreign policy is a great example of this. Candidate Obama explained how, rather than end his fight in Afghanistan, he would take the War on Terror beyond the Pakistani border. He's certainly done that. According to the Bureau of Investigative Journalism, as of July 2013, between 411 and 890 innocent civilians had been killed in drone strikes.

Hope and Change, with the help of a network.

ENDNOTES

1   Alterman, Eric. *What Liberal Media?: The Truth About Bias and the News.*
    New York: Basic Books, 2003

2   Pew Research Center's Journalism Staff "How Different Media Have Covered
    the General Election" 10/29/08

3   "Who Joined Maddow, Olbermann at the White House?" Politico http://
    www.politico.com/blogs/michaelcalderone/1009/Who_joined_Maddow_
    Olbermann_at_the_White_House.html 10/22/09

4   Shea, Danny "Keith Olbermann Suspended from MSNBC Indefinitely Without
    Pay" Huffington Post http://www.huffingtonpost.com/2010/11/05/keith-
    olbermann-suspended_n_779586.html 11/05/10

5   Dana, Rebecca "Slyer Than Fox: The Wild Inside Story About How MSNBC
    Became the Voice of the Left" *The New Republic* http://www.newrepublic.
    com/article/112733/roger-ailes-msnbc-how-phil-griffin-created-lefts-fox-
    news 3/25/13

6   Walsh, John "Al Franken is a Big Fat Phony" Counterpunch http://www.
    counterpunch.org/2005/05/04/al-franken-is-a-big-fat-phony/ 5/04/05

7   Steinberg, Jacques "Now in Living Rooms, the Host Apparent" *New York Times*
    http://www.nytimes.com/2008/07/17/arts/television/17madd.html?_r=0
    7/17/08

8   France, Louise "I'm not a TV anchor babe, I'm a big lesbian who looks like
    a man" *The Guardian* http://www.theguardian.com/lifeandstyle/2009/
    feb/08/rachel-maddow-american-television 2/7/09

9   Rispo, Vito "Obama Wins Ad Age's 'Marketer of the Year'" Ad Savvy http://
    www.adsavvy.org/obama-wins-ad-ages-marketer-of-the-year/ 11/05/08

10 Cockburn, Alexander "The Rand and Rachel Show" CounterPunch http://
    www.counterpunch.org/2010/05/21/the-rand-and-rachel-show/ 5/21/10

11 Fenley, Sean "Rachel Maddow Defends US Drone Program on Howard Stern"
    Dissident Voice http://dissidentvoice.org/2012/04/rachel-maddow-defends-
    the-us-drone-program-on-howard-stern/ 4/16/12

12 Maddow, Rachel *Drift: The Unmooring of American Military Power* Crown.
    2012

13 Davis, Charles "Rachel Maddow and Conservatism, the New Liberalism" Al Jazeera http://www.aljazeera.com/indepth/opini on/2012/04/20124713211145294.html 4/15/12

14 Prashad, Vijay "Victor's Justice Bedevils the new Libya" *The Hindu* http://www.thehindu.com/todays-paper/tp-opinion/victors-justice-bedevils-the-new-libya/article4049134.ece 10/31/12

15 Shupak, Greg "Libya and Its Contexts" *Jacobin* http://jacobinmag.com/2013/09/libya-and-its-contexts/ 9/2/13

16 Forte, Maximilian *Slouching Towards Sirte: NATO's War on Libya and Africa* Baraka Books 2012

17 Sadeghi, Shirin "Rachel Maddow vs. the Islamic Republic of Iran" Huffington Post http://www.huffingtonpost.com/shirin-sadeghi/racial-maddow-vs-the-isla_b_3067595.html 4/12/13

18 Borger, Julian and Dehghan, Saeed Kamail "Iran unable to get life-saving drugs due to international sanctions" *The Guardian* http://www.theguardian.com/world/2013/jan/13/iran-lifesaving-drugs-international-sanctions 1/13/13

19 Ioffe, Julia "Ezra Klein: The Wise Boy, A Tale of striving and success in modern-day Washington" *New Republic* 2/12/13

20 Sheth, Falguni "In America, Journalists 'Push Back': The Magnificent Hypocrisy of Toure http://translationexercises.wordpress.com/2013/02/06/in-america-journalists-push-back-the-magnificent-hypocrisy-of-toure/ 2/17/13

21 Greenwald, Glenn "MSNBC host mimics Fox News' bullying jingoism" *The Guardian* http://www.theguardian.com/commentisfree/2012/aug/24/msnbc-host-mimics-fox-news 8/24/12

22 Davis, Charles "'Unconditional allegiance is for machines, not people" False Dichotomy by Charles Davis http://charliedavis.blogspot.com/2011/07/unconditional-allegiance-is-for.html 5/6/11

23 Serwer, Adam "Is Israel Responsible for the Occupy Crackdowns?" *Mother Jones* http://www.motherjones.com/mojo/2011/12/blumenthal-greenberg-israel-occupy-crackdowns 12/7/11

24 Serwer, Adam "Time to redefine the term 'pro-Israel'" *Washington Post* http://www.washingtonpost.com/blogs/plum-line/post/time-to-redefine-the-term-pro-israel/2011/03/04/AGM3iGBH_blog.html 5/25/11

25 Serwer, Adam "Time to redefine the term 'pro-Israel'" *Washington Post* http://www.washingtonpost.com/blogs/plum-line/post/time-to-redefine-the-term-pro-israel/2011/03/04/AGM3iGBH_blog.html

26 Ruebner, Josh *Shattered Hopes: Obama's Failure to Broker Israeli-Palestinian Peace* New York: Verso 2013

27 Sheen, David "A year in review: Anti-African racism and asylum seekers in Israel" +972 Magazine http://972mag.com/a-year-in-review-anti-african-racism-and-asylum-seekers-in-israel/ 5/29/13

28 Blumenthal, Max *Goliath: Life and Loathing in Greater Israel* Nation Books 2013

29 Hitchens, Christopher "Pakistan is the Problem" *Slate* http://www.slate.com/articles/news_and_politics/fighting_words/2008/09/pakistan_is_the_problem.html 9/15/08

30 Hayes, Christopher *Twilight of the Elites: America after Mediocrity* Crown 2012

31 Ciccariello-Maher, George *We Created Chavez: A People's History of the Venezuelan Revolution* Duke University Press 2013

32 Deboer, Freddie "The Tryhards" *New Inquiry* http://thenewinquiry.com/essays/the-tryhards/ 8/31/12

33 Byers, Dylan "Liberal Media and Obama's Second Term" Politco http://www.politico.com/blogs/media/2012/12/liberal-media-and-obamas-second-term-150823.html 12/2/12

34 Coates, Ta-Nehisi "How the Obama Administration Talks to Black America" *The Atlantic* http://www.theatlantic.com/politics/archive/2013/05/how-the-obama-administration-talks-to-black-america/276015/ 5/20/13

35 Harris-Perry, Melissa "How Barack Obama is like Martin Luther King Jr." *The Nation* http://www.thenation.com/blog/how-barack-obama-martin-luther-king-jr 1/17/10

36 Reed, Adolph *Class Notes: Posing as Politics and Other Thoughts on the American Scene* New Press 2000

37 Harris-Perry, Melissa "Black President, Double Standard: Why White Liberals are Abandoning Obama *The Nation* http://www.thenation.com/article/163544/black-president-double-standard-why-white-liberals-are-abandoning-obama 9/21/11

38   Robin, Corey "Melissa Harris-Perry: Psychologist to the Stars" http://
coreyrobin.com/2011/09/23/melissa-harris-perry-psychologist-to-the-
stars/ 9/23/11

39   http://ohtarzie.wordpress.com/2013/01/07/a-real-shill-the-nations-ari-
melber-thenation-katrinanation-arimelber/ 1/7/13

40   Greenwald, Glenn "GE's Silencing of Olbermann and MSNBC's Sleazy Use if
Richard Wolffe" *Salon* http://www.salon.com/2009/08/01/ge/ 8/1/09

41   Horn, Steve "MSNBC Leans Forward Into Running Native Ads Promoting
Fracking" Desmogblog http://www.desmogblog.com/2013/11/04/msnbc-
leans-forward-running-native-ads-promoting-fracking 11/4/13

42   Stelter, Brian "Voices from Above Silence a Cable TV Feud" *New York Times*
http://www.nytimes.com/2009/08/01/business/media/01feud.html
7/31/09

43   Perlstein, Rick "Why Conservatives Are Still Crazy After All These Years"
Rolling Stone http://www.rollingstone.com/politics/blogs/national-affairs/
why-conservatives-are-still-crazy-after-all-these-years-20120316 *3/16/11*

44   Arria, Michael "The Idiocy of Demonizing Bradley Manning: An Interview
with Civil Rights Lawyer Chase Madar" Motherboard http://motherboard.
vice.com/blog/chase-madar-interview-bradley-manning 2012

45   Dixon, Bruce Joy Ann Reid, Melissa Harris-Perry as Prosecuter and Cop, Go
After Snowden, Wikileaks, and the First Amendment Black Agenda Reporter
http://www.blackagendareport.com/content/joy-ann-reid-melissa-harris-
perry-prosecutor-cop-go-after-snowden-wikileaks-second-amendment
7/3/13

46   Gosztola, Kevin "MSNBC Doesn't Cover Bradley Manning's Statement
or Guilty Pleas At All" *Firedoglake* http://dissenter.firedoglake.
com/2013/03/02/msnbc-doesnt-cover-bradley-mannings-statement-or-
guilty-pleas-at-all/ 3/2/13

47   Sirota, David "What Happened to the Anti-War Movement?" Truthdig
http://www.truthdig.com/report/item/what_happened_to_the_anti-war_
movement_20130905 9/5/13

INDEX

Medium Blue

Born Under a Bad Sky

By Jeffrey St. Clair

"Movement reporting on a par with Mailer's Armies of the Night"—Peter Linebaugh, author of *Magna Carta Manifesto* and *The Many-Headed Hydra.*

These urgent dispatches are from the frontlines of the war on the Earth. Gird yourself for a visit to a glowing nuclear plant in the backwoods of North Carolina, to the heart of Cancer Alley where chemical companies hide their toxic enterprise behind the dark veil of Homeland Security, and to the world's most contaminated place, the old H-bomb factory at Hanford, which is leaking radioactive poison into the mighty Columbia River.

With unflinching prose, St. Clair confronts the White Death in Iraq, the environmental legacy of a war that will keep on killing decades after the bombing raids have ended. He conjures up the environmental villains of our time, from familiar demons like James Watt and Dick Cheney to more surprising figures, including Supreme Court Justice Stephen Breyer (father of the cancer bond) and the Nobel laureate Al Gore, whose pieties on global warming are sponsored by the nuclear power industry. The mainstream environmental movement doesn't escape indictment. Bloated by grants from big foundations, perched in high-rent office towers, leashed to the neoliberal politics of the Democratic Party, the big green groups have largely acquiesced to the crimes against nature that St. Clair so vividly exposes.

All is not lost. From the wreckage of New Orleans to the imperiled canyons of the Colorado, a new green resistance is taking root. The fate of the grizzly and the ancient forests of Oregon hinge on the courage of these green defenders. This book is also a salute to them.

Available from CounterPunch.org and AK Press
Call 1-800-840-3683
$19.95

Weaponizing Anthropology

By David H. Price

The ongoing battle for hearts and minds in Iraq and Afghanistan is a military strategy inspired originally by efforts at domestic social control and counterinsurgency in the United States. *Weaponizing Anthropology* documents how anthropological knowledge and ethnographic methods are harnessed by military and intelligence agencies in post-9/11 America to placate hostile foreign populations. David H. Price outlines the ethical implications of appropriating this traditional academic discourse for use by embedded, militarized research teams.

Why We Publish CounterPunch

Back in 1993, we felt unhappy about the state of radical journalism. It didn't have much edge. It didn't have many facts. It was politically timid. It was dull. *CounterPunch* was founded. We wanted it to be the best muckraking newsletter in the country. We wanted it to take aim at the consensus of received wisdom about what can and cannot be reported. We wanted to give our readers a political roadmap they could trust.

A decade later we stand firm on these same beliefs and hopes. We think we've restored honor to muckraking journalism in the tradition of our favorite radical pamphleteers: Edward Abbey, Peter Maurin and Ammon Hennacy, Appeal to Reason, Jacques René Hébert, Tom Paine and John Lilburne.

Every two weeks *CounterPunch* gives you jaw-dropping exposés on: Congress and lobbyists; the environment; labor; the National Security State.

"*CounterPunch* kicks through the floorboards of lies and gets to the foundation of what is really going on in this country", says Michael Ratner, attorney at the Center for Constitutional Rights. "At our house, we fight over who gets to read *CounterPunch* first. Each issue is like spring after a cold, dark winter."

YOU CANNOT MISS ANOTHER ISSUE

Name _____

Address _____

City _____ State _____ Zip _____

Email _____ Phone _____

Credit Card # _____

Exp. Date _____ Signature _____

Type of Subscription: ☐ Gift ☐ Renewal ☐ New Subscriber

Mail check, money order, or credit card info to: CounterPunch P.O. Box 228 Petrolia, CA 95558. All renewals outside the U.S. please add shipping: $20.00 per year for postage, for Canada and Mexico; all other countries outside the US add $30.00 per year. The information you submit is confidential and is never shared or sold. Please give us your phone number, so that we may contact you in case of any questions with your renewal, or if there is ever a problem with your subscription.

☐ 1 year, print **$55**
☐ 1 year, email **$35**
☐ 1 year, both **$65**
☐ 1 year, reduced* **$45**
☐ Supporter **$65**
1 Year, Either

Mail Renewals to: P.O. Box 228 Petrolia, CA 95558
1 (800) 840-3683 or 1 (707) 629-3683 www.counterpunch.org